CRIME AND PUNISHMENT IN EARLY MODERN EUROPE

PRE-INDUSTRIAL EUROPE 1350-1850

General Editor: Dr Geoffrey Parker,
Reader in Modern History, University of St Andrews

PRE-INDUSTRIAL EUROPE, 1350–1850 is a series of historical studies which provides an introduction to the central themes of European economic and social history in the pre-industrial age. Each volume has been commissioned from a leading British, European or American scholar, and each presents a synthesis of the latest research, both published and unpublished, on a selection of critically important subjects related to the theme of the series, which is the gradual erosion of the traditional agricultural society of medieval Europe by a number of influences, chief among them the growth of capitalism.

By 1850, a new society had emerged in Europe, one that was capable of accepting and adjusting to the machine age. But it would be wrong to believe that industrial change caused this new society; on the contrary, the prior erosion of the traditional society and its values was an essential precondition of rapid industrialisation. It is therefore a matter of some importance to understand how fundamental social changes came about in Europe (and nowhere else) in the five centuries before 1850. By focusing attention on the key areas of change, this series aims to provide an explanation which will be of interest to scholars, students and the general reader.

1. POVERTY AND CAPITALISM IN PRE-INDUSTRIAL EUROPE
   Catharina Lis and Hugo Soly
2. CRIME AND PUNISHMENT IN EARLY MODERN EUROPE
   Michael Weisser
3. DEATH AND DISEASE IN PRE-INDUSTRIAL EUROPE
   Paul Slack
4. THOU SHALT NOT: THE CHRISTIAN CHURCHES AND SOCIAL CONTROL
   Bruce Lenman and Geoffrey Parker
5. BROADSHEET AND CHAPBOOK: POPULAR LITERACY AND POPULAR LITERATURE
   Peter Burke
6. ARISTOCRACY AND SOCIAL CHANGE IN PRE-INDUSTRIAL EUROPE
   Charles J. Jago

CRIME AND PUNISHMENT IN EARLY MODERN EUROPE

MICHAEL R. WEISSER

Associate Professor of History,
University of South Carolina

THE HARVESTER PRESS

This revised edition published in Great Britain in 1982 by

THE HARVESTER PRESS LIMITED

Publisher: John Spiers
16 Ship Street, Brighton, Sussex

First published in 1979 by The Harvester Press Limited

British Library Cataloguing in Publication Data

Weisser, Michael R.
    Crime and punishment in early modern Europe.
    (Pre-Industrial Europe, 1350–1850).
    1. Crime and criminals – Europe – History
    2. Punishment – Europe – History
    I. Title
    364'.94   HV6937

ISBN 0-7108-0365-6

Printed in Great Britain by
Photobooks (Bristol) Ltd.,
Barton Manor, St. Philips, Bristol

TO THE MEMORY OF
WILLIAM E. WEISSER

CONTENTS

PREFACE

This book marks the first attempt to treat the history of crime and punishment as a comprehensive whole. There have been numerous studies published about criminal law and punishment, but they usually make only scant reference to the question of crime. Likewise, studies of criminality are rarely placed within a legal or judicial context. Yet consideration of both issues allowed me to discern certain patterns and developments that might otherwise have remained hidden from view. The reader may object to this attempt to tie crime and punishment so tightly together. Each had its own logic, its own pattern of development independent of the other. This is indeed true, but such a conception is one approach to the problem, while my conception is another approach to the same problem. I believe them to be equally valid.

This is not to say that I consulted other authorities in vain. Some of the most venerable and traditional works on the subject proved to be valuable and indispensable references, providing facts and concepts that every student of the subject should know. The *History of the English Criminal Law* (London, 1948–56) by Leon Radzinowicz has lately received a bad press in some quarters, but it is unlikely that any of its critics will produce such a comprehensive and wholly-researched work. Of course it must be used with caution, but the same could be said of any encyclopedia. Rusche and Kirchheimer's *Punishment and Social Structure* (New York, 1939) is no longer mentioned in bibliographies, but the authors charted out many of the conceptions about crime and punishment that scholars in the field have yet to appreciate or discuss. I consulted many other valuable works and note those of particular importance in the bibliography. I cite the above works to draw attention to the fact that many pieces of important, but traditional scholarship have been ignored or abused in the pell-mell rush of social historians to open the crime archives.

Without realising or intending it, this book early on became a collaborative effort. Published material dealing directly with crime is still scarce, and it was necessary to consult many friends and colleagues in order to fill both theoretical and factual gaps that exist in the available literature. I would like to thank some of the persons who aided me during the research and writing of this project, beginning with the most important collaborators.

Scholarly prefaces often conclude with a brief note of thanks to the author's spouse. I would like to reverse the traditional procedure and thank my wife Susan first, because she contributed to this book in so many ways. Simply speaking, I could not have written it without her help. I would like to thank the editor of this series, Geoffrey Parker. He first suggested the idea of this book to me, patiently awaited its arrival, carefully edited the copy, and cheerfully saw it through to print. I would also like to thank my good friend Emanuel Chill, who genuinely knows this subject in a profound and thorough manner. I owe as well a great debt to Edward Malefakis, who has been a kind and intelligent friend through the years. His own work does not deal with the problems raised here, but it has none the less served as a model for my own research and writing. My colleague and friend Harry Cliadakis also proved to be an important collaborator in this work. He patiently listened to my ideas and offered suggestions and criticisms. Finally, John Walsh, Randolph Starn and Richard Kagan all read the entire text with great interest and care.

I would like to list some of the persons who were generous in their advice and knowledge during the course of this project. This includes Marvin Becker, Natalie Davis, Jonathan Dewald, Martin Fleisher, Eric Foner, Daniel Klobes, Thomas Laqueur, David Ringrose, Hilel Salomon and Irwin Scheiner. My former colleague Randolph Starn provided his inimitable brand of luncheon company while I first pondered my ideas about crime, and later read the manuscript at a crucial stage. My parents, Jean and Saul Weisser, provided a sylvan retreat where my ideas were put into concrete form.

Resources for this project were provided by the Educational Foundation of the University of South Carolina and by the Chairman of the History Department, Professor John Sproat.

PREFACE TO THE SECOND EDITION

The original text of this book was written in 1977, at a time when historical studies of crime were just coming into fashion. Precisely because of the absence of specialised research on so many areas of the subject, I made a point of noting the highly speculative nature of some of my ideas. In the following several years, a great number of new works appeared, some of which bolstered my hypotheses, others presenting a different point of view. Since my intention was to introduce readers to the problems in the field and create more interest in this particular branch of historiography, I am pleased that so many new additions to the literature have been produced. The purpose of this second edition is to highlight the new works as well as to revise at critical points where new information has become available.

Since the publication of the first edition, I have also continued my research in the field, and have consequently incurred new scholarly debts and intellectual obligations. I wish to thank in particular John Langbein, who took the time to help me sharpen my ideas on aspects of criminal procedure. I am also indebted to Dr. Jan Stepan, Librarian at The International Legal Studies Center of The Harvard Law School. I can never adequately repay the support of Dr. Ivan Sipkov, Chief of the European Law Division at The Library of Congress. Samuel Popkin has tirelessly urged me forward in my work and R. Randall Bridwell and William J. Quirk continue to provide their unique vision of the relationship between law and human development. Just as with the first edition, this book would never have appeared again without the love and encouragement of my sweet wife.

INTRODUCTION
THE PROBLEM OF CRIME AND PUNISHMENT

SOCIETY first creates thieves, wrote Sir Thomas More, then punishes them for stealing. This brief but profound statement from the pages of *Utopia* forces us to remember that there has always existed a curiously symbiotic relationship between the criminal and society. It is not so much that society tolerates crime; rather the structure of modern society inevitably creates situations and circumstances in which crime occurs. Like the poor who are always with us, crime cannot be made to go away. And like a study of poverty, which should tell us a great deal about the accumulation of wealth, so a study of crime should illuminate a wide variety of non-criminal activities in society.

The purpose of this work is essentially twofold: to analyse some aspects of the transformation of early modern European society through the perspective of criminality; to analyse the incidence of crime and the behaviour of criminals as a measure of how early modern society was being transformed. It is hardly necessary to resort to statistics in order to demonstrate that crime occurred on a very frequent basis during the early modern period. Everyone believed this to be the case, and such beliefs were concretised into action on many distinct fronts. The early modern period witnessed, among other developments, the first sustained debate on the nature of crime, the first serious revision of criminal law codes, the first rationalisation of judicial and prosecutorial activity, the first

1

creation of a rational system of punishment, and the first appearance of the police force. This coincidence of events certainly had many causes and motives beyond the simple question of an increase in the crime rate, but at least we can say that the issue of criminality had finally come into its own.

From a certain point of view this would not be a difficult essay to write. The contemporary literature on criminal activity, punishment systems and legal developments is abundant, and nearly every observer of the contemporary scene made reference to one aspect of the problem or another. Moreover latter-day historians have lately discovered that crime is a verifiable social trend and that criminal data can be utilised to buttress any number of hypotheses concerning social developments in the early modern period. Therefore, in the place of detailed grisly descriptions of spectacularly fiendish crimes, or pseudo-scientific investigations of a particularly crime-prone segment of the population, we can now turn to quantitative studies that link the incidence of crime to demographic movements, harvest levels and even temperature trends.

Yet despite this new-found objectivity, modern studies of criminality share a common bias with earlier works in the field. Scholars still consider crime to be a form of aberrant behaviour, but the motivation for this aberrant behaviour has taken on a different dimension. The aberration is viewed either positively or negatively, but its incidence is a 'barometer' of social upheaval and its forms are a conscious or unconscious reaction against harvest failure, unemployment, war, or any combination of socio-economic traumas. This approach utilises evidence about crime as a springboard for the study of social crisis and the analysis of specific criminal activity becomes subsumed in a more general examination of the social problems or social tensions involved. This perspective colours the historical view of criminals as well. The great majority of lawbreakers, it is thought, will always turn back to more lawful forms of activity once the conditions that provoked their criminality cease to exist. Criminal behaviour and the motives of individual criminals are thus seen as a reaction to some other development or set of circumstances. The life-long, professional criminal does not occupy a specific category of activity and is rarely analysed on his own terms. No doubt, many people who commit criminal offences, petty and serious, are victims of social forces far beyond their understanding and control. And we should also be mindful of the fact that many sorts of activities were defined as illegal acts, as Michel Foucault says, 'to criminalize the customs of the poor in the name of work discipline,'[1] or for other political and social motives. Nonetheless, this still leaves the question of crime disguised or obscured by other factors presumed to be more important; a judgement motivated more for reasons of latter-day historical or political consciousness than for anything related to the specific context of the crimes themselves.

In this essay, crime is seen as a basic social activity with its own internal logic and historical development. This viewpoint presents a number of intriguing problems, but an essay that followed more traditional historiographical paths would tell us very little about the social context in which crime occurred. It is possible, however, to discern an enormous and intricate web of social and economic relationships that underlay criminality at all times, momentary shifts in its frequency notwithstanding. Crime statistics for the early modern period are incomplete, but they demonstrate beyond a shadow of a doubt that crime was an integral aspect of European social development, occurring more frequently than either births or deaths. Punishment systems ultimately adopted by European countries were another indication of the regularity of crime. Punishment reflected not only the whole scope of social relations in society, but indicated a general awareness of how crime both threatened and facilitated those relationships.

The implications of these ideas when applied to the available data take us far beyond the usual parameters of historical discussion concerning the nature and significance of crime. Although crime is usually seen as an index of social distress, it can also be appreciated as an index of social development. An analysis of certain types of crime tells us about the problem of unemployment, but other types of crime illustrate the nature of work. Crime was sometimes indicative of family disintegration; at other times criminal activity was an essential component of a stable family life. We will develop all of these concepts and others in great detail over the course of the narrative, but one last general point should be made at this time. It is imperative to analyse crime in its social context for the following reason. Society often determines in an *ex post facto* fashion what activities constitute criminal behaviour, and the nature of crime as it is formally defined often has little connection with its original function or cause. Indeed the legal description of a criminal act often bears little resemblance to the actual criminal event. Even the judicial procedure utilised to determine the extent of criminal activity becomes a charade, a ritualised set of motions that has no relationship to the crime or the criminal. Consequently the alternatives between legal and illegal activity never existed in any clear-cut fashion, and people rarely made behavioural choices on the basis of theoretical, legal postulates, if they were even aware of their existence. The history of crime is far more than a compilation of criminal statutes and a statistical compilation covering the number of times that each statute was broken.

With the exception of several brief essays on specific situations or criminal activities, there still does not exist a single historical study that deals with the issue of crime as a typical event in the history of society. The reluctance or inability of historians to study the significance of crime in all its social dimensions has resulted in an emphasis upon certain types of criminality, such as mob violence and religious crime, and this has resulted in the further neglect of the issue of crime itself. This book is an attempt to redress that historiographical and conceptual imbalance. It will utilise descriptions and sources that have no apparent reference to crime, yet tell us about the environment in which many types of crimes were committed. It will also draw upon information covering criminal activity, use the information to illuminate noncriminal activities, and then examine those activities to illustrate the social context in which crime occurred. Finally this essay will rest upon the notion that criminals were not marginal social elements, but were an integral part of the European population. Further, it is supposed that many persons who committed crimes did not do so in a casual fashion, but rather as a conscious, premeditated form of livelihood and occupational activity. As the demands and pressures upon that population changed over the course of the early modern period, such changes could be witnessed within the context of crime and criminal life.

The gradual shift from feudalism to industrial capitalism exerted profound pressures upon all segments of the European population. Every single aspect of European society was affected to some degree by the inexorable transition from one type of social system to another. The purpose of this *Harvester* series in the history of pre-industrial Europe, 1350–1850, is to chart the results of that long-term historical development from various social perspectives, and to compare the transformation of a particular social phenomenon to the transformation of society as a whole. The purpose of this book is to compare crime to society within that historiographical context, bearing in mind both the limitations and possibilities afforded by such a comparison.

The eventual emergence of industrial societies meant the obliteration of previously-existing modes of behaviour, social customs, traditions and attitudes. This was largely the result of vast changes in the geography, scale and structure of the human community. As these changes occurred over time, the pattern of human interaction within the community was transformed as well. Different economic and social relations were imposed upon the population and this was reflected even in the manner by which persons signified their understanding of the situation. New forms of work reflected new forms of economic organisation, new forms of communication reflected new social dimensions. Historians believe that the essence of the shift from feudalism to capitalism lay in the new patterns of human interaction – the scope of this interaction as well as its organisation. Historical accounts of the transition from feudalism to capitalism that fail to note this phenomenon or explain its implications are far from complete.

For many reasons, crime is the quintessential activity that draws people together. A crime consists of inflicting some form of injury upon another person. The injury can take many different forms, sometimes neither tangible nor material. The attack may consist only of a verbal insult, resulting in 'loss of face', or it may result in damage only to property. However, regardless of the actual specifics of the crime, the important factor is that a victim or his representative must be produced who can claim some kind of loss. This last point is the crucial element in the communality of criminality, for according to accepted definitions (e.g., that of the *Oxford English Dictionary*), a crime is an activity that is *punishable by law*. This definition assumes the existence of an entire legal and political structure erected around the question of crime – a structure whose description and analysis will of course form a focal point of this work. Yet the essential conception to be understood here is that the illegality of criminal activity presupposes a vital social dimension. Crime does not occur on an isolated basis, and for that reason is subject to legal restraints imposed upon it by the whole society.

Since every crime involves at least two persons in the roles of attacker and victim, we can be quite certain that in many instances there had been some degree of social contact previously. This is not to say that the criminal and his prey knew one another personally, although this was true in certain types of crime. Rather the individuals maintained a prior social relationship in a wider, more abstract context; they were both part of the milieu in which the crime took place. Or at least they represented social elements that had distinct and real social relationships. We will see that Europeans often postulated the existence of a 'professional' criminal class as opposed to the 'casual' criminal population. The latter group consisted of those persons who resorted to crime occasionally out of a sense of desperation, yet never considered themselves criminals in any generic sense. The former group consisted of those individuals who truly led a life of crime, whose entire existence was spent in planning and effecting all sorts of capers. However, while this dichotomy may have served important social and cultural conventions of the period, we must understand it more in terms of the attitudes it represented than the reality it attempted to describe.

In point of fact, nearly all crime is 'professional' in the sense that it occurs within a milieu understood and frequented by the criminal himself. The motives for crime vary enormously but the physical and social circumstances in which it occurs almost inevitably reflect the life patterns and environment of the individuals involved in criminal acts. When a man is hungry he will steal bread – an historical syllogism that admits of no easy or practical solution. Yet the bakery that he enters as a thief in the night is more than likely the same establishment that he enters as a customer by day. A workingman who needs to supplement his meagre wage in order to survive will likewise steal and sell the tools or materials from his own shop. These crimes may be spontaneous and unplanned, but they do reflect a long and careful analysis of a particular social milieu. More to the point, they tell us some very important aspects about the social environment that turned ordinary individuals into criminals.

The role of the professional criminal is sometimes more difficult to understand, but it none the less yields very crucial information about social affairs. The professional criminal literally makes his living from crime. If he is successful it becomes his occupation and his career in every sense of the word. He does not resort to criminal activity on a sporadic basis but spends all his time operating within a criminal context. Yet he too understands the necessity to execute the rigours of his craft in ways that reflect the social reality of his existence. If he adopts certain disguises for effecting an illegal entry into exclusive premises, this tells us what types of individuals ordinarily operated in those circumstances. If the professional criminal confines his activities to certain neighbourhoods, this tells us a great deal about the living patterns and social structures of the community itself. The professional criminal understood clearly that his success was based upon disguising his true intentions by adhering to lawful behaviour as closely as possible. We must therefore pay close attention to both aspects of his activity.

The extent to which all crime was premeditated is a fundamental reason for understanding and appreciating the social context in which crime occurred. But what about the incidence of actual criminal activity? After locating the milieu of crime, the next logical step would be to chart its frequency. This type of data forms an important part of any analysis of criminality, but it is subject to several analytical shortcomings. First and most important is the issue of unreported crime, both in its legal and social dimensions. The size of the 'black' figure has generated considerable dispute, and there is simply no way of telling how much crime was 'hidden' within criminal statistics. Throughout the early modern period, the impetus for criminal prosecution often rested entirely with the victim who had to bring the crime to the attention of the authorities and present all relevant evidence and witnesses. Legal recourse was consequently a time-consuming and often fruitless method for settling disputes and this was an inhibiting factor in the reportage of crimes. Furthermore, until the nineteenth century, there was no comprehensive judicial or police system operating in any country of western Europe. Consequently, criminal statistics were often a function of the vagaries of local procedure, and frequently tell us more about the structure of the judicial system than they enlighten us about actual patterns of crime. Certain types of crime were handled in one court, another judicial institution held jurisdiction over other sorts of crime, and a third or fourth separate authority held sway over other forms of criminal activity committed in still other places.

In certain parts of Spain, for example, crimes committed in a local settlement were heard in the courtroom of the nearby municipality. Crimes committed outside the village, in open pasture or woodland, were heard in the courtroom of the royal police. Specific crimes, such as murder or treason, could only be tried in national courts located at the royal chanceries. This confused jumble of penal jurisdictions was characteristic of every early modern European society. In France, for instance, Castan has remarked that, 'an exhaustive inventory of the organizational structure, at the level of the kingdom, or even at the provincial level, would be neither comprehendable nor realizable.'[2] Thus, the patchwork system of criminal administration prohibits us from assuming that criminal statistics emanating from one place were representative of the whole.

It was also the case that certain social factors frequently militated against the reporting of crime in any comprehensive fashion. Frequently communities would settle criminal disputes through informal mechanisms if they felt that the judicial system was a means of imposing controls over the entire community from the outside. Within the community certain segments would react in a similarly negative fashion to a legal system that could be used to consolidate the authority of one group over another. Punishment also played an important role in the degree of reporting of crime. Judicial systems that placed a premium upon reconciliation of attackers and victims, or systems that allowed a maximum of judicial and legal manipulation by the parties involved literally invited the reporting of every crime, no matter how trivial. On the other hand, judicial systems that contained severe and certain penalties were inevitably occupied in dealing with a small proportion of the committed offences.

It is also important to analyse the social implications of criminal statutes. As society became more thoroughly organised, this was reflected in one respect by the increased specificity and detail of criminal codes. Over time criminal statutes became both wider in scope and more precise in description, denoting new forms of illegal activity while detailing their variations to greater degree. An understanding of the relationship between crime and society must involve a penetrating analysis of these codes, both in their judicial as well as normative functions. Criminal codes tell us not only what constitutes illegal activity, but also what actions and activities are important and worthy of protection. The shape and content of criminal statutes are also a potent indicator of the extension of political power through various levels of society. Sometimes, however, these codes must be used with extreme caution, and the scholar should be aware of the myriad motivations behind the promulgation of various criminal laws. In Spain, for example, the breeding of mules was prohibited under severe penalties after 1512, because a sterile animal would eventually deplete the national stock of horses and deprive the army of a necessary resource in time of war. The law was no longer enforced after 1630, although it remained on the statute book long after that date. Instead the Crown began to collect income taxes in a much more vigorous manner, and now prosecuted individuals for fiscal rather than breeding violations. Similar examples of statutory changes abound in the history of criminal law, and serve as reminders of the necessity of considering the social context of every aspect of European criminality.

There are certain types of crime, however, that, despite their intrinsically social character, will not be discussed in this work. However we have included a bibliographical listing for these subjects. Perhaps the most frequent types of crime in Europe were those that occurred during riots, rebellions, revolts or revolutions, specifically crimes of arson, criminal trespass, assault and mayhem. Large-scale urban lawlessness in Europe had a tradition and history that dated back to at least the fourteenth century and was first associated with the lower-class populations of medieval industrial centres in the North as well as in the larger cities of the Italian peninsula. Over the entire span of the Old Regime, however, urban disorders were usually less serious than the crime and violence associated with peasant movements. Indeed, many of the key events of the early modern period cannot be understood when lifted out of the context of rural disturbances that were occurring at the time. For example, the consolidation of the French ruling house in 1598 was in reaction to rural rebellion, as would be its dissolution some two centuries later.

The criminality associated with incidents of rural or urban mass violence lies beyond the scope of this work if for no other reason than the manner in which such crimes were treated by the authorities. Regardless of the rhetoric employed, participants in such affairs were not considered criminals in the ordinary sense of the word. Their only criminal act was unlawful assembly, and once the field was cleared they were rarely charged with specific crimes. Sometimes a ringleader was seized and brought before the authorities, but he was inevitably charged with treason as opposed to any particular criminal act. Only in the nineteenth century did the police begin to investigate rebellions and riots on an individual basis, collect information and compile criminal dossiers. Until that time the criminal aspect of a rioter's behaviour was entirely incidental to the manner in which the authorities reacted to his crime.

A second type of crime that will not be analysed in this narrative embraces the category of religious offences, particularly crimes of bewitchment like witchcraft, sorcery, black magic and demonology. Many reasons have been advanced for the existence of sorcery and other forms of demonological possession in western Europe. Studies have shown, however, that it is nearly useless to generalise over the motivations behind witchcraft activity, since the forms of behaviour and the modes of prosecution varied widely from place to place. Yet despite the great varieties of witchcraft practice and prosecutorial energy, it is clear that the punishment of religious crime necessitated the tacit or active support of the local community. Consequently, the history of this particular form of criminality leads to an examination of certain social questions that are only marginally related to the question of crime. In fact, like the analysis of mob behaviour, it is often convenient and necessary to dispense with the criminal aspects of the problem altogether.

This brings us to a third category of crime that will be excluded from this work for similar reasons. Although political crimes and conspiracies affected no more than a handful of individuals over the course of the early modern period, they were some of the most notorious and publicised crimes of the day. In reality, most political crimes had little connection with the real motives that lay behind the accusation. In many instances the punishment of political offenders, often individuals of high standing, served as a 'proof' of the equality of justice under arbitrary political regimes. In other instances political conspiracies were 'uncovered' as a convenient explanation for political ineptitude at the top. For these reasons and others it would be impossible to analyse political crimes within a framework designed to look at criminality in general terms.

Despite the exclusion of many different types of crime, we are still in a position to consider most of the illegal activities that constituted the bulk of European criminality during the early modern period. This includes many crimes that were horrendous and notorious, and many criminals whose brutality lived on in popular consciousness for generations after they had allegedly committed their fiendish deeds. Yet this criminality, despite its occasionally sensational aspects, was still ordinary crime. First, it did not occur only within the context of other, non-criminal conflicts. In this respect, it differed from all the crimes mentioned previously. Second, the perpetrators of these crimes were considered and treated as criminals. They were not thought to be rioters, religious fanatics or political dissenters, and no matter how macabre or mundane their activities, they were not responsible for events or activities beyond the scope of their personal behaviour. Third, and most important, society did not recognise these crimes to be exceptional and no special procedures were established for dealing with their perpetrators. It was recognised that such crime occurred on a normal, systematic basis and this led to the creation of normal, systematic methods of punishment. Just as society became more organised, so crime became more regularised and punishment more normalised. In essence the most frequent forms of European criminality reflected the most frequent forms of social relations existing at that time.

The basic criminality of early modern Europe can be grouped conveniently into two broad types: crimes against persons and crimes against property. This division is often arbitrary and flies in the face of the actual events surrounding a specific criminal event. In fact, as we are well aware, many crimes result in damage both to property and persons, regardless of the original intent of the perpetrator. Yet this division between the personal and the material as objects of a criminal attack formed the basic structure of most criminal codes. If we adopt it here as well it allows us to focus upon two distinct types of conflict that stood at the root of most crime. Crimes against persons – assault in its various physical and non-physical forms – reveal the existence of specific forms of social tensions that often cannot be resolved without recourse to violence or abuse. The occurrence of such crime in a particular locality alerts us to the possibility that certain forms of communication within a community no longer function as originally intended, or that certain types of conflict can no longer be resolved in the usual, non-violent manner. This problem is not as simple as it first appears. In certain environments assault included various forms of verbal abuse and other, non-violent attacks upon members of the community. These attacks were treated by the authorities no differently from actual, physical assaults and they were representative of a set of social norms and conventions that disappeared over the course of the early modern period. In certain societies and communities we will find that random, physical violence was endemic to certain types of social relations, occurring on a basis so frequent as to indicate another set of social conventions that have since disappeared. In other situations, at other times, personal violence appears to be taboo; it occurs in only the most serious and infrequent circumstances, and it involves a much greater sense of injury and loss.

As for crimes against property, such offences reveal certain types of economic circumstances and conflicts that would not emerge from a study of other forms of data. For example, it is usually thought that the first hint of peasant resistance to landlords can be seen in the refusal to pay taxes or dues. However there were places in Europe during the early modern period where peasants delivered all obligations to their lords as scheduled, meanwhile engaging in constant theft from seigneurial domains. As in instances of violent crime, there was a wide variation in the extent and type of crimes against property in early modern Europe. In some areas crimes against property were directed almost exclusively at members of the peer group. This profile reflected, among other things, the structure of the community and the nature of social relations. In other places attacks on property in its various forms became an aspect of class protest embracing aspects of a covert war waged by the poor against the rich. These types of crime also reflected the scope of certain social relations within early modern society.

Despite regional and chronological variations, European criminality in the early modern period consisted of about 50 per cent crimes against property, roughly 30 per cent crimes of violence against persons, and about 20 per cent miscellaneous offences, the latter often relating to the specific structure of the judicial system in force at that time. Criminal statistics from fourteenth-century Italian cities, fifteenth and sixteenth-century rural England, seventeenth-century Spain and eighteenth-century France all point to the overwhelming preponderance of larceny in its varied forms. No matter where we look, at whatever period or particular environment, a decidedly similar situation emerges in the general crime profile: Europeans simply could not resist taking things that belonged to others. At certain times this type of crime may have become a little more prevalent, at other times its incidence would very slightly subside. But those short-term trends could not obscure the simplicity of the overall statistic. Stealing was an activity so common as to be nothing less than banal.

Most scholars would seek immediately to correlate the trend of larceny with other social indices, and this is an essential aspect of the analysis of criminality. But there are other, perhaps more intriguing implications of this evidence that will be briefly mentioned here and then explored in detail in later chapters. Theft presupposes not only the activity of a thief but the existence of an item of such value as to warrant its unlawful removal. Consequently our primary interest revolves around the identity of the stolen item and then the identification of the locality from which it was taken. If the data could be collected, one might be tempted to draw up a geography of European theft, and then analyse the shifts in this geographical profile over time. This analysis would reveal many significant facts about the structure of European society, points of transit, zones of exchange and areas where goods were concentrated in large numbers and for different purposes. For example, patterns of theft are crucial clues to understanding the development of urban centres. Thieves tended to concentrate their activities in areas where disposable goods were readily available. The most popular sites of theft therefore were markets, usually held in the open and located adjacent to rapidly-expanding urban neighbourhoods. The pattern of larceny also varied according to the basic structure of the particular urban economy. As we shall see below, crime statistics in seaports were somewhat different from criminal patterns at inland points, and levels of criminality often changed in response to changes in the scope and rhythm of the urban economy.

The rural areas of Europe, while also displaying a preponderance of theft in the overall pattern of criminality, tended to show distinct types and methods of theft depending upon the environment and location of the particular settlement. In villages located near cities petty theft was often the predominant form of crime, and it consisted of burglary and the taking of luxury items from private homes. This profile reflected a number of significant factors regarding the location and social structure of these settlements. It demonstrated the existence of a constant traffic between the village and the nearby urban centre, because items of great value could be disposed of or 'fenced' in the city, whereas their unexplained presence in the local hamlet would attract attention to their new owner. The victims in such cases of theft were often city dwellers who had acquired a country retreat, and furnished it in the style to which they were accustomed. Yet they were often absent from their homes for many weeks at a time, rendering the premises much more vulnerable to illegal entry.

As one moved further away from urban centres, the pattern of rural settlement tended to change, and this resulted in a somewhat different profile of rural crime. In rural villages lying beyond any immediate contact with the city, theft more frequently took the form of trespass and the taking of farming articles, such as tools, planting stakes, fence posts and other, semi-manufactured articles that could be put to immediate use. Often the land upon which the criminal trespassed belonged to an absentee owner, but these thefts also occurred on lands of local residents. Thus criminality in more isolated rural settlements tended to be an aspect more of intra-class relations rather than an activity reflecting inter-class disputes. This was indicative of the existence of a certain degree of social cohesion in rural settlements whose social structure was not yet directly affected by the impact of economic and political forces emanating from the urban centre.

In the furthest, most remote rural zones, larceny was exemplified by the activities of the bandit or highwayman. The existence of bandit gangs alerts us to the location of frontiers, borders not so much in a geographic context as in the ability of political authorities to exert real control over their theoretical patrimonies. Traditionally bandits operated in mountain zones because they were precisely the places where police would find it most difficult to track them down. At the same time bandit activity was also a sign of the location of important trade and commercial routes, for it was along such thoroughfares that bandits operated most frequently. A poignant example of the connection between bandits and highways is provided by the case of the Santa Hermandad tomb in the Puerta de Marches pass in the mountains of central Spain. The Santa Hermandad, the rural police force of pre-modern Spain, had reputedly built a tomb in this remote mountain pass for holding the corpses of highwaymen caught and killed along this particular route. The remains of the tomb were discovered around 1900, confirming a century-old hypothesis that the route through the Puerta had originally served as an important route of commerce from central to southern Spain.

One can also project a number of interesting historical inferences based upon the identities of persons involved in various forms of rural and urban larceny. In eighteenth-century Paris, for example, many of the felons convicted of theft were country dwellers recently arrived in the city and unable or unwilling to engage in legal labour under the prevailing wage structure of the period. A century later perhaps a majority of the criminal population of Paris were native born, indicating a possible shift in the type and extent of rural immigration to the city and perhaps a transformation in the urban economy. Significant analytical points also spring up in the study of rural criminals. There was sometimes a clear difference between the rural beggar and the rural transient; at other times they were one and the same individual or class. The attempt to classify begging as a crime has always led, then and now, to a blurring of such distinctions, when in fact they are quite important. Yet it is often just as misleading to establish too strict categories of social analysis based upon a settled versus transient life-style: the latter did not necessarily denote a less lawful type of existence than the former. Many tasks and activities in the early modern economy could not be accomplished except through constant movement of the workforce from place to place. In the course of such movements the distinctions between legal and illegal activities often became quite vague.

Alongside the usual correlations that can be developed between criminal trends and other social indices, we can also infer a great deal about social developments from a study of criminality in its own social context. In other words, crime has a logic of development as a social activity in and of itself. Of paramount importance in this narrative will be the necessity to establish the social functions of crime. And this task can be accomplished notwithstanding the enormous gaps in evidence and lack of reportage that exists in all criminal documentation. Let us bring this perspective to bear in an examination of the second most common form of crime, namely violence between individuals, or simple assault.

It is almost a truism of criminology that most persons commit violent assaults against members of their own social class. This analytical syllogism leads scholars inevitably to view such incidents as prime evidence of social tension or social crisis within a particular community or population group. However, certain types of assaults that occurred frequently in pre-industrial Europe were manifestations of inter-class conflict in a sense other than that exemplified by mob violence. One frequent form of assault involved attacks by masters upon servants, a type of incident that became public notice only on rare occasions because legal statutes often recognised the right of the master to enforce discipline in harsh terms.

Another related form of physical violence occurred between craftsmen and apprentices, a type of crime indicative of the social relationships that formed around certain kinds of pre-industrial work. We should also mention the most prevalent but least understood form of violence that contained as well certain elements of inequality among the parties: namely family violence and particularly physical abuse visited by parents upon their children. This is a very difficult issue to analyse in traditional criminological terms, but it none the less probably constituted the most frequent form of physical assault in pre-industrial Europe.

A mention of family violence is an opportune place to raise the matter of unreported crime in a different context than that discussed above. Later in the narrative we will discuss evidence that demonstrates the increasing impoverishment of the criminal defendant population over time. Yet the extent to which the poor were involved in criminal proceedings was not only a reflection of the increasing class nature of crime, but also indicated an important shift in the structure of European criminal justice systems. In the feudal period, the criminal justice system rested upon the initiation of a legal process by the victim or his associates, and only on rare occasions did the force for prosecution emanate from the officers of the law. Consequently, just as early judicial systems were open to personal manipulation by the parties to the case, so they also operated for the benefit of those with material or social importance within the local community. These 'personalised' judicial systems, as we shall see, encouraged participation and involvement, but only on the part of those who could afford to get involved. As a result objective criminal statistics for the early period are hardly a precise measure of the incidence of certain types of crime. Our estimate of the proportions of basic criminal activities is in part projected with this factor in mind.

Although assault and larceny accounted for upwards of 85 per cent of all ordinary crimes committed (and reported) in Europe during the pre-industrial era, there were still a wide variety of other types of illegal activity occurring on a common and everyday basis. A significant portion of this criminality consisted of violations relating to the structure of the judicial process, or the manner of punishment and crime control. Chief among these crimes were the various forms of obstruction of justice, including the many different types of accessories to felonious acts, particularly larceny. Certain thefts could not be effected without an accomplice who would be responsible for hiding or moving the stolen goods from one location to another. In particular, commercial theft and smuggling necessitated a whole chain of conspirators and often involved entire communities in the illicit movement of contraband commodities. Another important criminal offence involved the violation of the terms of a sentence or parole, and this frequently occurred when punishment included exile or banishment. A key Dickensian character was Magwitch, who appears in *Great Expectations* as a convicted felon who violates his sentence of perpetual banishment and returns covertly to England. Crimes of this sort are an important indicator of the extent to which the judicial system was able to enforce its own laws.

The mention of Magwitch can serve to introduce the second basic theme of this essay, since his activities served as a reminder throughout the novel of the wide spectrum of social relationships that existed between the legal authorities and the society that they were supposed to protect. Just as crime was part and parcel of European society, so punishment was also a common event, especially when it was meted out on an organised, systematic basis. In fact it is impossible to discuss crime during the early modern period without discussing punishment, because as Sir Thomas More realised, they were two sides of the same problem. Nobody ever imagined that all criminals might be caught and punished, but the existence of punishment could at least make clear the seriousness of crime.

The early modern period marked the consolidation of Roman law and the systematisation of punishment, and these developments involved the novel recognition that different types of offences should be punished by different methods. The beginnings of a logical system of punishment in Europe also marked the recognition on the part of society that crime had a certain social logic. It was not enough to lump all offenders in a single category, since each particular offence had a rationale all its own. For these reasons it cannot be assumed that the emergence of a systematic criminal punishment process in the early modern period was only a response to increased criminality or only a reflection of the development of the national state. For the consciousness of European society was not oriented only toward an awareness of crime *per se*; rather it became focused upon the realisation that different types of crime existed in certain specific forms. Essentially, the development of modern justice and punishment systems was preceded by the appearance of a vague philosophy of criminality, and then by the first tentative attempts to define crime in ideological, class terms. Consequently, in dealing with this problem, we must distinguish between concepts of justice and concepts of punishment. The former concepts were the motivating force behind changes in courtroom procedure, and they reflected such factors as the growth of state power and the perceived need to control the increase in crime. The latter concepts derived, however, from mental attitudes about the nature of criminality, and this was more a reflection of social developments in the society at large.

Changes in the criminal justice system occurred within specific political contexts. It is impossible to separate legal procedures from political procedures, because the legal system always becomes a crucial mechanism for reinforcing and extending the ideology of the dominant political power. More importantly, the ideology of the European political system was often maintained through direct recourse to the criminal justice system. Criminal codes placed great emphasis upon deference to authority, respect for persons of social standing, obedience to the King's law. To a certain extent, these ideological issues even overshadowed the importance of criminal codes in terms of their procedural structure. Theoretically, the courtroom served as an open forum where the guilt or innocence of a particular individual could be established indisputably before his peers. Yet in reality, the courtroom functioned as a form of theatre, with the representative of the central, political power – the magistrate – playing a leading and often histrionic role. The magistrate appeared attired in his robes and surrounded by a variety of assistants all playing deferential and highly circumspect parts in the drama. The judge became the high priest of justice, and the similarity was intended and constantly renewed.

The ability of the magistrate to exercise such potent theatrical powers while enforcing the law was amplified by the nature of early modern criminal codes. In theory, these codes covered nearly every type of criminal offence, and also prescribed the requisite punishment for each illegal act. Yet the sentences were no more than theoretical postulates that hinted at the seriousness of a particular crime. In terms of actual punishment, early modern criminal codes allowed the magistrate to exercise the widest possible discretion. More importantly, until the sixteenth and seventeenth century, criminal codes contained next to nothing covering judicial procedure, and it was in this area that the magistrate could exercise truly extraordinary legal and melodramatic powers.

Legal reformers of the early modern period faced two critical problems. We will deal with these issues at great length in later chapters, but they can be summarised here as follows. First, they had to draw up a criminal code that reflected the extension of central authority in comprehensive terms. Second, they had to devise a method for instituting strict procedural behaviour in the courtroom and throughout the entire criminal justice system. In essence a system implied some form of accountability for the individuals who were chosen to oversee its activities. At the same time, the system had to operate in such a manner as to ensure equality before the law. These two tenets – equality and accountability – were the capstones of the reformation of criminal law and procedure during the early modern period. Yet the reformers also had to be careful to strike a fine balance between the need of the system to render fair judgements and the need of the system to preserve both the appearance and the reality of authority – the latter an especially delicate task as the criminal code became an essential means to consolidate class hegemony. At the same time legal reformers also realised that to go to the other extreme and attack the institution of authority in any fundamental manner would breed very grave social and political consequences. Thus criminal law reforms were always more advanced in rhetoric than in reality. Arbitrary authority would be checked in theory but order through the use of authority would be maintained in fact.

The work of legal reformers was also related to attempts to devise new and more rational systems of punishment. Part of the impetus for revising punishments stemmed from the attack on arbitrary political power, of which an obvious manifestation was the wholesale and indiscriminate use of torture in criminal procedure. But the first changes in the form of punishment occurred as a result of the growing awareness of the social context in which crime occurred and a shift in the general consciousness regarding social questions. This was largely because of the increase in poverty among the European masses and the consequent attempts to curb the numbers and movements of poor persons in every country of western Europe. A second factor that influenced the development of new punishment systems was the growth in the size of the urban population. Now it was necessary to utilise punishment as a method of social discipline, if only because rich and poor came into such intense contact within the urban milieu.

The most fundamental revision of punishment systems occurred, however, at the end of the early modern period; this consisted of the introduction of the penitentiary. Earlier, as theories of labour productivity gained ground, all sorts of experiments were conducted using convict labour to lower the general wage rate and consequently raise profit levels. Thus by the seventeenth century the poorhouse had been merged with the workhouse and the forerunner of the modern prison came into being. This new penal institution, known as the house of correction, had little impact upon the European labour market. Yet the same institution ultimately had an enormous influence upon the development of criminal punishment. The concept of incarceration would lead directly to the idea of fixed, determinate sentences that could be adjusted exactly to fit the particular crime. This was seen as an efficient alternative to corporal punishments that had previously been meted out with scant attention to distinctions between crimes. The arbitrary nature of earlier punishments could now be replaced with a logical and precise method of penalties that more easily fit modern conceptions of rational justice and law. The penitentiary system thus became a precise means of retribution visited by the entire society upon the individual who had shown himself incapable of adapting to lawful norms. The idea of equality before the law had now been extended to include equality in terms of punishment.

The link between crime and society was cemented in

its modern form with the appearance of the police. For the first time, an institution had been created for the express purpose of dealing with criminal offenders on the most immediate terms. This meant that modern methods of punishing criminals would now be complemented by modern methods for controlling crime. The new police forces of Europe bore little resemblance to their earlier counterparts. They were organised along bureaucratic lines and followed strict rules of procedure. Previously police dealt with crime in an intermittent fashion, deploying at certain crime-ridden points or reacting to specific criminal incidents. The hallmark of the modern police force, however, was continual surveillance of the entire population and crime prevention on a comprehensive basis. To attain those ends police bureaucracies soon developed centralised criminal archives that became repositories of information of all kinds to be endlessly sifted and studied. This development marked the final event in the transition from pre-modern to modern crime, for modern criminality would provoke the science of criminology.

CHAPTER 1
THE SOCIAL ENVIRONMENT OF CRIME AT THE BEGINNING OF THE EARLY MODERN PERIOD

THE overwhelming physical and social reality of the medieval world was isolation, and this factor predetermined the contours of all human activities, including crime. Human contact was limited both in degree and kind; social customs and economic patterns reflected the lack of everyday exchange and communication. People lived in small, separate units, either tiny rural agglomerations surrounding a château or parish, or in undeveloped urban centres containing specialised populations that served the needs of particular institutions. The isolation of population centres had as its social obverse a high degree of personalised contact within each little milieu. Often the population of an entire village was comprised of kin, particularly if the settlement could trace its origins to an original pioneer family that had moved away from a larger hamlet some time in the past. In the medieval city, every little neighbourhood formed by the boundaries of the parish, held persons who could claim some formal social, familial or occupational tie with everyone else residing in that part of the town.

The influence of this isolated and personalised existence can be traced in every important function of early modern society. It was certainly a compelling factor in determining the modes of work and the relationship between workers, as well as between employers and their helpers. In the towns it was exemplified by the institution of the guild, a self-enclosed group of entrepreneurs whose structures fostered a perpetual co-mingling of personal and business affairs. The ethos of the guild – familiarity and exclusivity – was bolstered by the apprenticeship system. This method of recruitment guaranteed that business affairs would be carried on within a narrow, strictly-defined social context, since it meant that labour could be drawn from within the family or a circle of close friends and associates.

The personalisation of work relationships in the countryside took somewhat different forms. Frequently it was characterised by the various communal activities that marked much of the rural labour of the Old Regime. In particular the rural community often organised some form of communal pasture and local rights over the commons were jealously guarded from outside interference. In France the communal pasture was considered to be an inviolate possession of the whole peasant community and disputes with local nobility usually centred around this question. In Spain common pastures (*dehesas*) were among the first privileges extended by medieval monarchs to peasant communities that developed during the course of the Reconquest. There were also many forms of communal farming, encountered less frequently in areas tied to national grain markets, but more prevalent in the remoter rural zones. All of these activities reflected a close connection between work and social relations.

This socio-economic relationship was most intense within the context of family labour, a common form of economic enterprise in both the urban and rural sectors. Few business enterprises, located either in the rural or urban milieu, were conducted outside the immediate family circle, nor did many important social relationships develop beyond the family base. The family was not only the employer of first resort for relatives and kin; it was usually the most frequent source of employment for outsiders as well. The appearance of the *domestique* in a French household, or the Spanish counterpart, *criado*, did not necessarily signify that the employer possessed any substantial wealth. Indeed one of the most conspicuous social phenomena of the Old Regime family structure was the frequency of servants within the home. This held true in both the urban and rural environment and from the top to nearly the bottom of the social hierarchy. One might conjecture, therefore, that outside of farming, domestics comprised the largest single occupational category in the active population of early modern Europe. Naturally many types of crime would occur within that context.

But aside from these generalities, the social structures of the early modern period affected criminal patterns in very specific ways, particularly in terms of the social makeup of the population. Let us look first at the composition of the urban sector. The town was the centre of trade and commerce. It was usually located at the nexus of important trade routes and its population included those persons who directed regional and national trade. Perhaps the classic example of the commercial basis of urban life at the close of the Middle Ages is provided by the development of Venice, whose fortunes reflected its location at the hub of Mediterranean and overland trade between East and West. As a result of trading opportunities, most larger towns also became early centres of manufacture. The development of craft industries was based upon the proximity of a market network available only in the more important urban centres. By combining trade and industry, towns also became centres of consumption, drawing in both raw, industrial products to satisfy the needs of local manufacture and raw and finished foodstuffs to satisfy the dietary needs of the urban population. In all three respects – trade, industry, consumption – early modern cities differed quite markedly from rural population centres, and these differences affected the composition of the population as well as the entire scope of social activities.

The extent and diversity of the population and its social composition was governed foremost by the size of the particular town. The largest cities, those counting more than 50,000 persons at the end of the Middle Ages, contained the most heterogeneous populations both in terms of occupation and social class. Western Europe had only eight or nine cities of this size in the fourteenth century: Milan, Florence, Genoa and Venice in Italy, Cordoba, Granada and Seville in southern Spain, and Paris, London, Ghent and Bruges in the North. We know very little about life in the Moorish cities of Spain, although Islamic texts talk of an urban environment of immense cultural vitality and intense economic activity. As for the largest Italian cities, it is clear that as early as the fifteenth century these huge urban concentrations contained nearly every type of social and economic element that we would associate with the population of the most modern metropolis. At the same time the largest cities also contained the greatest number of poor and, in fact, the indigent population of the largest cities was sometimes greater than the total population of smaller towns. This collection of human refuse was most conspicuous in the large cities for a variety of reasons, chief among them being the availability of resources, the possibility of part-time employment and the inability of municipal authorities to control social problems in the face of such staggering numbers.

In the North, the urban centres of London, Paris, Bruges and Ghent also contained large and diverse populations. Like the Italian cities, these northern centres also held great numbers of poor and working-class elements that had been attracted to the town in search of alms or work. The active population of all the large cities was divided between the craft, commerce and service sectors. Craft workers were usually engaged in textiles, the typical early modern industrial activity. There were also a wide variety of luxury articles fashioned by craft workers, most of them demanded by the luxury clothing trade and consisting of articles fashioned from silk, leather and lace. The proportion of the active population engaged in crafts was roughly similar to the proportion of the working population engaged in trade, an indication of the complementary nature of these two activities in the early modern economy. In fact it was impossible to draw a strict line of division between the two occupational sectors. Many merchants were often successful craftsmen who had developed a large trade, hired other craftsmen and thus detached themselves from active participation in the industrial process. However, when a momentary slump occurred in the business cycle, smaller merchants would discharge several of their employees, scale down the size of their operations and resume their original place in the workshop. Upon the resumption of trade and industrial activity the scenario would be reversed.

The service sector was the predominant occupational category in all the largest cities and was comprised of so many general vocational groupings that it could be broken down into several large sub-categories. In seaports like Venice and Genoa a large part of the service population centred its activities around the docks; this included the construction, loading and sailing of ships. Many workers floated from one occupation on the wharves to another, a continual movement that was accentuated by the cyclical nature of early sea commerce. Perhaps the largest sub-category of service workers comprised the various types of construction labour, an occupation that probably claimed the greatest number of workers in the urban service sector outside of those engaged in personal domestic work. Little is known about the working conditions of construction labourers, beside the fact that their wage was usually the base salary upon which all other wages were figured. But it is clear that, with the exception of a small minority of skilled craftsmen, the construction industry experienced a very rapid turnover of manpower, and it was difficult to exert any degree of control over this part of the urban workforce.

There were other service occupations that played an important role in functioning of the urban economy. Most important in this respect were the numerous service tasks that were related to food provisioning, including the labourers who worked in the food markets throughout the city and the cattle drovers and cross-country teamsters who brought provisions to the urban centre from the surrounding countryside. For every greengrocer and other retail specialist engaged in the food trade there were numerous odd-job employees whose activities were crucial for the daily distribution of foodstuffs to the urban population. Employment in this sector of the service trades was probably more regular than in the construction industry, but it was still a type of labour that brought a minimal wage and was subject to all sorts of seasonal and short-term fluctuations.

Although the service sector contained all the marginal occupations, seemingly unimportant when compared to the prestigious mercantile professions, service tasks were essential in maintaining the rhythms of urban life in the early period. In fact the service occupations may have been the most important activity in the early modern urban economy, since the labour performed there cemented together and rationalised the functioning of the other two sectors. In a society completely lacking in automation techniques and labour-saving devices, every type of economic activity became labour-intensive and every aspect of work needed a large complement of workers in order to accomplish the necessary labour. The service sector contained an enormous population that could always be called upon immediately to perform a wide variety of unskilled or semi-skilled jobs. The specialised activity of craftsmen and businessmen had its necessary counterpart in the dull, repetitive labour of the masses.

The factor that most distinguished craft and commercial activities from service activities was that the former fostered economic as well as social relationships to the labour market, while in the latter case, the economic factor was the more important. Under the guild system, for example, social factors played an important role in determining aspects of the economic situation. Yet it was precisely this social dimension that was lacking in most service occupations in the medieval city. In the case of most service occupations labour was rewarded or calculated on the basis of a cash wage. As a result a true labour market developed earliest in this sector, a system that embodied the concept of wage employment and its attendant corollary, unemployment. Consequently it was within this population and this vocational context that most of the early urban crime occurred. The service population included the poorest segment of the urban mass. It was also most directly exposed to the negative effects of economic crisis, and the cyclical employment structure militated against the development of any social cohesion that could have alleviated the consequences of economic distress. Finally, and most important, competition in its most brutal and blatant sense was the hallmark of the labour situation in the service sector. Since immigration to the city tended to outpace the supply of jobs, a buyer's labour market existed on a continual basis, giving the workers little control over the conditions of labour or of their lives.

The competition for jobs, upon which everything else depended, was a day-by-day struggle that usually went against the best interests of the labouring population. Moreover any brief equilibrium that might be achieved between the contending forces could be instantly upset, either through new waves of immigration to the city or through an abrupt turnaround of the business cycle due to diminishing commodity demand. Consequently there was always a great deal of social tension manifested amongst the service population and it was in this sector that crime became almost a normal part of life. Criminal activities served as a means of survival in periods of extreme labour competition, particularly in periods characterised by sudden economic reversals. Later in this chapter we will examine the types of crime that illustrate more concretely the social context in which this part of the urban population existed.

Alongside the largest European cities were a greater number of smaller urban centres, containing between 25,000 and 50,000 persons in the period following the Black Plague. There were perhaps twenty such cities, including Padua, Verona, Naples, Rome and Palermo on the Italian peninsula, Barcelona, Lisbon and Valencia in Iberia, Rouen, Toulouse, Bordeaux and Lyon in France, and Cologne, Nuremburg and Prague in the German areas. There were also a series of smaller cities, holding upwards of 10,000 persons; this group included the remaining important provincial centres, university towns and ecclesiastical settlements in western Europe. In these smaller towns the division of the active population was different from that in the largest cities, and this was reflected in the existence of different social relations, as well as in the development of a different profile of crime. In smaller cities the commercial, industrial and service sectors all contained about the same proportion of the active population, and this reflected a more rudimentary economic base. Many of these towns had developed around one basic industry and few persons could be found in the city whose occupation did not directly relate to this particular economic activity.

The diminution in the proportion of the active population engaged in service occupations usually also meant that the particular town attracted fewer poor persons. Cities not yet grown to great size were frequently able to control the movement of poor persons in a more efficient manner, and such communities did not contain the conspicuous wealth of larger towns that was often an object of plunder by the poor. In smaller towns a larger part of the service population was made up of persons who worked in adjacent farmlands owned by the municipality. This type of labour was less sporadic than many other service activities, and it resulted in a greater sense of cohesion and security amongst the poor.

It is quite obvious that the largest medieval cities were centres of crime not only because they contained so many poor persons but because of the nature of work available for most of the lower-class population. Only the largest European cities – Venice, Florence, Paris, London – supported both an important mercantile and craft population, and the economic and social activities of this commercial and industrial elite provided most of the employment possibilities for the service sector. In the long run the growth in the wealth and power of urban, elite groups would provoke the construction and redecoration of urban dwellings, create a demand for domestics and other casual servants and produce vast quantities of disposable wealth that could support all sorts of part-time and marginal activities. It was the existence of the mercantile community that created the milieu in which the urban poor could exist and established the basic conditions that shaped their lives.

Crime was a significant response of the poor to conditions that confronted them in the urban environment. It was a means of survival; it was also a method of protest. Although cities were much smaller than they are today, the density of population was quite high, and persons of all social classes lived in close proximity to one another. An entire neighbourhood could be traversed in several hundred metres, and one could move from the wealthiest to the poorest segment of the town in a matter of minutes. Moreover it was not uncommon for many poor persons to be seen around the city's wealthier districts; nearly every household of means was serviced daily by all sorts of lower-class tradesmen and service people. Thus there was no lack of opportunities for thieves and other criminals to observe the habits and possessions of potential victims in the course of appearing to do an honest day's work.

A somewhat fanciful but nonetheless representative picture of urban criminality during this period is pro-

vided in a chapter of Benvenuto Cellini's *Autobiography*.[1]
At the time Cellini had been commissioned to work some
precious stones for Pope Clement and the jewels were
in his goldsmith's studio alongside his apartment. One
night, while Cellini was involved with his female servant,
a thief entered the studio but was scared off by the growls
of a watchdog. He managed to get away with the clothes
of Cellini's apprentices, who had apparently slept through
the entire incident. Since every event in the *Autobiography* was explained from the egoistical perspective
of the author there is good reason to doubt the total
validity of this particular tale. But even allowing for a
degree of exaggeration, the description of the crime gives
us some important information about urban crime at
this time. It is clear, for example, that as early as the
fourteenth century, an urban underworld existed in
which news of Cellini's hoard would be spread and provoke an attempt to steal it. Furthermore the thief was
prepared for his activity; Cellini was sure that he had
earlier entered the house, posing as a goldsmith, in order
to survey the premises and guess the location of the
gems.

Theft in the urban milieu was an inter-class affair. The
rich possessed many items of value that were easily disposable even in a compact and limited urban environment. Most urban thieves were recent arrivals to the city
or their mode of existence forced them to move frequently
from place to place. Yet in every town they had accomplices who observed possible situations for committing
crime and passed along this information. The habits and
possessions of the urban elite were probably catalogued
by the many domestic servants employed in almost every
well-to-do household, and this information was circulated
in lower-class neighbourhoods. The rich depended upon

the poor to serve them in a variety of personal ways, and the poor could turn this service to their own advantage from time to time.

Just as incidents of larceny involved lower-class elements in great numbers, so urban violence tended to be more the province of the middle and upper classes. This was at least the profile of urban violence in *reported* crime. No doubt there was a great deal of sporadic violence amongst the lower classes, but the nature of the judicial system and the structure of the urban community operated against the reportage of such crime. On the other hand, armed and organised violence often characterised the political and social relations of the urban elite. Family feuds, so often the theme of novels set in the Renaissance, were a constant source of lawlessness in the urban environment. This was particularly true in the Italian towns where political elites often engaged in small civil wars in order to determine the political future of the city.

Along with murder the only other crimes that could result in capital punishments for the upper classes involved various sexual offences, usually committed in a violent context. In fact sexual crime was the 'prerogative' of the upper classes throughout the entire early modern period. Given the social values of the urban elite, a serious sexual crime was probably the only form of criminal behaviour that the upper classes would not condone among themselves. Indeed the stability of the elite, a stability based upon marriage and inheritance, was more directly threatened by rape than by murder. Moreover the luridness and violence of many sexual crimes lived on in the popular consciousness and the impact of the crime went far beyond the importance of the act itself. Consequently a sexual crime was the type of criminal act the authorities could prosecute on an individual basis and thereby slake the thirst of the masses for equal justice before the law.

Let us now turn to the situation in the rural sector and then return to the profile of urban crime in order to make some general comparisons between the two environments.

Despite the fact that the countryside contained the overwhelming bulk of the European population in the early period, our information about social relations and criminality is much more sketchy than in the case of the urban milieu. Yet the basic typology of the rural settlement was similar to the urban centre since the size of a particular village also determined the economic and social profile of the local population. The size of a country hamlet was first predicated upon its location and its history. Some settlements were originally annexes of larger villages, particularly in areas like southern Spain or eastern Germany that were still considered frontier zones at the close of the Middle Ages. These hamlets were often quite small and their development tied to the economic and social patterns of the parent settlement. Other rural settlements had been founded by an individual lord or an ecclesiastical institution, and the size of these populations often reflected the terms of settlement imposed upon the peasants by their master. Finally, as noted previously, some villages were outposts of cities, located within close proximity of the town, and containing homes of well-to-do city residents who even then felt the need to escape the city for the dulcet pleasures of a country weekend.

The size and social structure of the rural settlement was also determined to a great extent by land tenure patterns. Although many communal farming activities would continue to be carried out throughout the entire early modern period, this occurred in the face of a general movement toward the stratification of landownership. From the Middle Ages onward, private possession and use of farmland was the rule rather than the exception in the European countryside, and this pattern became even more apparent as the period wore on. The most important development in this respect was the extent to which land was owned by persons other than those who resided in the settlement. By the sixteenth century, perhaps half or more of the arable land in western Europe was held by persons or institutions not situated on that land on a full-time basis. This had resulted largely from the extension of seigneurial domains and the influence of regional and national urban markets upon the rural sector. Absentee ownership – land in the hands of the Church, the aristocracy, the urban bourgeoisie, or a rich peasant who could afford to move into town – resulted in the removal of as much as half of the available land from direct exploitation by local residents. It meant that a majority of the rural population could earn a living only by labouring on the land of others. This accentuated social and economic divisions within the settlement itself. Let us look at these differences more concretely.

The basic socio-economic division within the rural population was characterised by the ownership or non-ownership of draft animals. An Old Regime rural family that could afford a team of oxen or mules usually possessed enough land or other resources to remain self-sufficient over the course of a year. But this was the minimal standard. In fact the individuals who owned draft animals, known as *laboureurs* in France (*labradores* in Spain), frequently controlled nearly all the farmland in a given community, either through direct ownership or various rental agreements. This landowning class in the village, moreover, rarely comprised more than one quarter of the local population and the proportion tended to diminish over time.

The remainder of the local population, with the exception of a very small professional group (cleric, doctor, shopkeeper, etc.), comprised the *manouvrier* class, those persons who owned little or no land and gained their subsistence by hiring themselves out to other persons. The size of this labouring population varied from village to village but its working conditions were affected most immediately by the extent of absentee holdings, the economic connections between the village and other population centres, and the diversity of the local economy. As cities grew in size and developed more intense economic relations with their surrounding hinterlands, this tended to siphon more of the labouring population away from working upon the farmland in the community and into various service occupations that helped maintain the connection between the local community and the urban centre. A whole portion of the village population would now develop independent of the organic structure of the community, tied instead to patterns and demands imposed upon the local community by the outside world.

The beginning of the early modern period saw the emergence of two service populations, one located in the cities and another located in the rural sector. The service population in the countryside was a creation of the city; it was brought about initially by the predominance of absentee landholding and was amplified by the economic and commercial inroads of the urban economy upon traditional rural life. The activity of this rural service population was no less essential for the rational functioning of the economy than was the activity of its urban counterpart. Their labour was essential during peak harvest periods when foodstuffs had to be gathered from the fields and distributed throughout the region in as efficient a manner as possible. They also performed important labouring services during momentary spurts in the urban economy when a sudden demand for raw industrial materials had to be met through increased production and exchange in the rural sector.

As in the case of the urban lower classes, a large proportion of the rural masses were the underemployed, labouring poor who worked on a seasonal basis and were at the mercy of economic and social forces far beyond their control. Just as the labour of the marginal service population in the city was a key factor in rationalising the urban economy, so the labour of this marginal population in the countryside was an essential ingredient for maintaining the economic rhythms of the rural sector. Likewise it was amongst this segment of the rural population that competition and social tension was most acute. It was also amongst this portion of the population that rural crime assumed important dimensions. As in the city the general conditions of work bred a social climate of insecurity and instability that inevitably provoked high levels of crime. Although the records from the period are far from complete they confirm the extent to which patterns of rural criminality were a direct product of this situation.

Like urban criminality, the basic profile of rural crime centred on the prevalence of larceny, a crime usually committed by poorer persons who lacked simple necessities of everyday life. The items most frequently stolen were food and clothing, along with an assortment of basic farm implements and tools. A labourer would find himself lacking a few poles for tying vines and would walk into a neighbouring field to lift them from another's vine-yard. Most stolen items were objects that could be consumed immediately by the family of the thief or passed easily from hand to hand without the possibility of being traced to the original owner. Jewellery and other luxury goods were rarely taken in incidents of rural larceny. They did not exist in great abundance, nor could they be effectively hidden or sold in the local community. Villages were too small and too cohesive to permit a successful thief to concentrate upon luxury items. Furthermore, communication between the village and the city was still infrequent and it was thus more difficult to take away purloined goods without attracting undue notice. The distance to town was too great to be negotiated quickly, the typical rural dweller was too unfamiliar with city mores, and his absence from the settlement would immediately provoke notice. Consequently, although poverty was the chief motivating factor in rural larceny, this activity took on a much different pattern than in the context of city life. It was usually confined to the theft of small items of limited value and it was often an intra-class rather than inter-class activity. The social structures of the rural community could allow for no other type.

There was also a great deal of simple and aggravated assault in the rural sector, and this offence was characteristic of both poor and more well-to-do community elements. As we shall see in the following chapter the legal system that operated at the beginning of the early modern period allowed individuals with means to bring every little grievance into the public arena. Consequently criminal rolls from this period inevitably list an enormous number of assaults and injuries involving middle and upper peasants, indeed far beyond their actual proportions within the local population. Often the legal system as well as the individuals themselves made no distinction between physical as opposed to verbal assaults, with the latter often provoking more frequent use of the legal system in order to gain recompense. A significant point to note here is that rural criminal violence occurred frequently on an individual basis.[2] It was not until later that criminal gangs began operating in the countryside, and the latent, group violence that often characterised social relations in the cities was almost completely absent from the rural milieu.

On the other hand non-violent rural crime was very frequently a family affair, and types of crimes were often determined by the structure of the family unit. The family involvement in larceny, for example, was indicative of the social utility of crime, as well as the necessity to use the family as a means of subterfuge in a small and watchful community. The most frequent criminal partnership within a family context involved brothers, but it was not uncommon for spouses to act together to involve children as accomplices in various criminal activities. Once certain types of crime had become part of the basic existence pattern of a part of the population, then family cooperation was essential for the success of any criminal activity, as well as for the survival of the family unit.

Although our evidence is quite meagre it is possible to construct a quantitative profile of urban and rural crime at the beginning of the early modern period. The urban data is extrapolated from punishment lists drawn up in the fourteenth and fifteenth centuries in northern Italian cities, while the rural profile concerns crimes reported in seigneurial domains around Lyon in the fifteenth century.[3] There are obvious problems with both sets of data: the former is more representative of punishment systems rather than of criminal trends, the latter heavily weighted in terms of the specific relations between peasants and lords. Yet evidence from other sources shows this data to be somewhat representative of criminality in the early period:

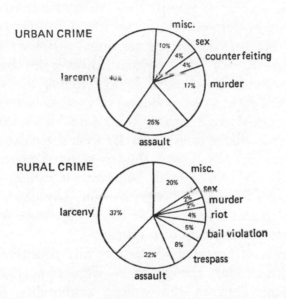

These charts demonstrate quite clearly some of the important differences between urban and rural criminality. Moreover some of the difference in the two profiles was due to the appearance of certain distinct forms of crime that could exist only in specific environments. Counterfeiting, for example, was an urban crime par excellence, and its occurrence reflected the fact that cities were already moving to a cash economy while the rural sector still exchanged most goods through the barter system. On the other hand trespass was a peculiarly rural crime, and particularly noticeable in areas dominated by seigneurial holdings. The urban evidence is probably disproportionately weighted in favour of murder while

understating the actual rate of assault. But these proportions again reflect the extent to which assault was much
more of an unreported crime in the urban milieu than
in the village community.

Other differences between urban and rural crime do
not show up in the quantitative evidence but were quite
important in demonstrating the social context of crime
during this period. The proportion of larceny in both
environments was fairly equal: however in the city it
often involved the theft of luxury items, while in the
countryside most stolen goods were various types of basic
commodities. Urban larceny tended to be an inter-class
affair, while village thieves usually took the possessions of
their peers. Finally, urban thieves were often transients
who could be out of town before their crime was uncovered. Most rural thieves, however, tended to remain
in the community, since their hasty departure would in
itself provide suspicion of a crime.

The rate of assault in both city and countryside was
also quite similar, though there were important social
distinctions between the violent criminality in both
sectors. Urban violence was often a group affair, the
motives very involved and often possessing historical roots.
In the countryside, however, assaults were usually individual affairs, involving only the attacker and his victim,
the motivation being both short-term in effect and trivial
in origin. Urban violence tended to occur between the
same two parties over extended periods of time, sometimes turning into feuds that embraced families and
neighbourhoods for generations. This was one reason
for the extremely high murder rate in many urban centres;
armed, premeditated violence usually results in a high
homicide rate. In rural settlements, on the other hand,
violence was rarely premeditated. It was almost always

confined to the briefest of outbreaks and rare that weapons besides sticks and stones were used. Many of the assaults reported to rural magistrates were nothing more than various forms of verbal abuse, including swearing at another individual in a public place or allegedly passing evil rumours throughout the neighbourhood. There were no end to such incidents in the city, though they were reported to the authorities on a much less frequent basis.

In summary we can say that while the profile of urban and rural criminality was quite similar at the beginning of the early modern period, there were very great differences regarding motivation and circumstances. These differences reflected the distinct social structure of the two environments as well as the different role that crime played in each milieu. The differences in criminality were also indicative of the extent to which these two environments, while beginning to become similar to one another, were still distinct social entities. Yet over time both environments would change and become even more similar, and these developments would have profound effects upon the nature of urban and rural crime.

CHAPTER 2

THE LEGAL ENVIRONMENT OF CRIME AT THE BEGINNING OF THE EARLY MODERN PERIOD

LIKE every other aspect of feudal society, criminal law and punishment reflected the isolation and localism of the age. Each feudal magnate claimed judicial competence over his particular realm; every feudal institution claimed legitimate authority to adjudicate some types of disputes. The multiplicity of jurisdictions reflected the absence of any effective, centralised authority; it also reflected the inability of early monarchs to extend their sovereignty in substantive, comprehensive ways. Invariably medieval kings were forced to grant concessions in certain areas in order to extend their power in other respects, and this type of exchange always militated against the development of effective state power. In particular, medieval monarchs were frequently willing to exchange judicial and legal authority in return for the ability to tap various sources of revenue and, in the long run, this pattern accentuated the welter of competing judicial patrimonies.

The dislocation of centralised judicial power was least extensive in England since the Normans forced the continuation and strengthening of public (royal) courts as a means of consolidating their conquest. However, in France the feudalisation of the ninth and tenth centuries resulted in the multiplication of judicial institutions and this development was even more intense in the German

51

lands. In fact one scholar has remarked that France was about 100 years behind England in the development of public judicial procedure and court organisation, while Germany lagged some 200 years behind France.[1] We might add that Spain probably remained at least a century behind Germany regarding the extension and rationalisation of a public court system. The reader should therefore bear in mind that any comparison between English and continental judicial procedure must allow for certain chronological discrepancies.

The absence of comprehensive criminal systems in Europe meant that local areas were often left to devise their own methods for controlling crime. Thus the fragmentation of legal authority brought about the growth of informal methods of criminal control that met the needs of various local populations. Although these local systems ostensibly followed general norms of legal and judicial procedure, traditions and practices more applicable to the particular social situation tended to predominate over the entire criminal justice process on the local level. Local methods of controlling crime usually incorporated a great many cooperative practices and also relied upon the entire civilian population to help maintain the peace. Aside from social circumstances, these political factors were also an important element in the maintenance of a private system of criminal law.

Despite a wide variation in local procedures, however, European feudal societies tended to adopt similar definitions of crime and punishment. This similarity stemmed from the backward state of economic and social relations throughout medieval Europe. Crime was considered only in its personal context: it was an illegal action, an injury, committed by one person against another. Consequently medieval criminal justice was a private affair, meant not so much to punish as to maintain stable social relations between parties of equal rank. In essence medieval criminal justice revolved around the idea of personal vengeance.[2] Therefore the plaintiff was usually in a position to control the entire process by which the defendant would be convicted, sentenced and punished. Legal procedures allowed the plaintiff ample opportunity to avenge his sense of loss without actually subjecting his adversary to the full force of the law. Punishments were often benign, designed to force the criminal to accept public responsibility for his acts as well as atone publicly for his behaviour.[3]

The distinction between what we are calling public and private criminal law must be examined in order to understand the later evolution of the criminal justice system in Europe. The issue can be described briefly but the reader should bear in mind that typical criminal procedure was far from actual criminal procedure; the prototype of a criminal process under either system was never followed perfectly in day-to-day judicial affairs. None the less some generalisations about private and public criminal procedure illustrate concretely the basic differences between the two systems.

In both private and public procedure a criminal case was usually initiated by the victim, who then became the plaintiff in the case. However, under the system of private law and accusatory procedure, the plaintiff remained the motivating force behind the entire procedure. He prosecuted the case, presented the evidence and testimony necessary to substantiate his claims of damages and even decided whether or not the defendant should be sentenced by the court. Once the victim felt that his injury had been avenged he could withdraw his complaint and the proceedings would end at that point. As we shall see, even private criminal proceedings contained a number of strict procedural points that had to be followed in the course of a criminal case. Yet the plaintiff was consulted at each turn and his option to withdraw his complaint gave him unlimited discretion over the entire event.

In public proceedings, on the other hand, the original suit filed by the plaintiff was the first and last moment when his actions would supply the motivation for continuing a case. Following his denunciation of the alleged criminal the entire procedure would be placed in the hands of outside authorities, who would now prosecute the case on behalf of the state rather than on behalf of a private individual. Consequently all discretionary authority was removed from the control of the plaintiff and, like the defendant, he became just another party to the case. Yet despite the obvious advantages of public procedure in the control of crime, it was a system as yet almost unknown in medieval Europe.

The existence of a private system for prosecuting crime was an important indication of the social factors that permeated all aspects of feudal life. The development of private law reflected first the ethos of equality that dominated the popular consciousness at all levels, as well as the absence of class-based values and social distinctions. Although legal historians have frequently disagreed on the exact nature of this issue there seems little doubt that some elements of ancient communalism had survived and even crept into medieval court procedure in England and elsewhere. This sense of equality meant that the legal system was structured to enforce peer judgements at all levels of feudal society. Knights of the realm might judge their vassals but they also sat in judgement of other knights. This limited sense of democracy within the legal system was particularly evident in France and Germany, where private feudal courts survived for a long period as important bulwarks against the spread of royal power.

The functioning of private criminal procedure was symptomatic of the weakness of coercive measures that lay behind the medieval criminal justice system. Any social group that had to enforce its statutes without resort to armed force consequently depended upon the willingness of all its members to share the burdens of law enforcement on an equal basis. This type of cooperation could only occur among persons of equal or near-equal status. One particular aspect of the medieval criminal system illustrates this point with great clarity. The feudal tradition of sanctuary was transformed into a quaint ideal by Victor Hugo and other romantic writers, but it none the less served an important function in the Middle Ages. Under feudal law a clerical institution could offer sanctuary to all those except persons with criminal records, traitors, heretics and individuals already convicted of the crime in question. The person to whom sanctuary was granted was allowed to remain on the premises for forty days, after which he could be removed by any possible means, including the burning of the hallowed structure to the ground. Sanctuary allowed an individual to escape from his pursuers or a local posse when he believed that he was wrongly accused of a crime. The grace period of forty days was considered long enough for word of the event to spread around the community, thus provoking the legally-constituted authorities to take action in the matter. But the true significance of the sanctuary, which ended by the fifteenth century, was that it demonstrated the extent to which criminal justice was often a private concern. The sanctuary allowed an alleged offender to escape his private avengers and ultimately seek refuge in public hands.

The private nature of medieval criminal law also resulted from the lack of a police force or other type of organised crime-prevention brigade. In England, the 'hue and cry' system served as a means of mobilising the community to take action against a suspected criminal, but it only functioned at sporadic intervals in some parts of the country and depended upon the watchfulness of private citizens who would set off the alarm. In Spain during the medieval period, local communities often formed *cuadrillas*, or town leagues, for the purpose of guarding common pastures against interlopers and maintaining vigils on the roads that connected the settlements. But none of these local expedients could or did assume the functions of a police force in the modern sense of the term. Many early governments supported small, mounted forces for the purposes of patrolling important thorough-fares and protecting travellers from highway bandits. One of the most famous of such patrols was the *Santa Hermandad* that was first established by the Catholic Monarchs as a mobile force within Castile. But effective police supervision of the entire population was hampered by difficulties of movement, the remoteness of many rural settlements and the unwillingness of early monarchs to spend the necessary funds. Consequently police protection was almost a local affair, a further factor promoting the development of private methods for settling criminal disputes.

The existence of a private system of criminal procedure during the Middle Ages also fitted the geographical contours of early settlements. Since most persons lived within the confines of a manor, or inside the walls of a small urban centre, crime prevention frequently took the form of various methods to promote internal security. After nightfall, access to the community was limited to local residents, and the appearance of any stranger in the darkness was usually cause for calling a general alarm. The feudal community thus possessed the legal right to segregate strangers and effectively control crime. We see manifestations of this practice in the frequent literary and historical references to the location and clientele of roadside inns in Europe. They were nearly always located out side the limits of the town or the village and nearly all the lodgers were strangers to the area in which the inn was located.

Perhaps the most instructive method for analysing the functioning of a private criminal justice system would be to follow a particular criminal case from its inception to the conclusion of the procedure.[4] We have chosen a very typical crime, an instance of simple assault, in order to concentrate upon the procedural rather than the sensational aspects of the process. This crime occurred in the village of Los Yebenes, in the province of Toledo in central Spain. The village fell under the jurisdiction of the city of Toledo, which meant that every criminal indictment came under the purview of the Toledan judicial system. Each criminal case had its inception in the local settlement but ultimately was resolved in the courtroom of the magistrate in the city. The case dates from 1624, long past what we consider the end of the feudal age. But private criminal procedure persisted in many areas of Europe long into the early modern period, and in this region of Spain it would characterise the criminal justice system until well into the eighteenth century.

The case was opened on 24 December when Juan de Pedro Alameda came to the home of the village notary and denounced Garcia Diego de Villareal and Juan de

Robledo for allegedly punching him as he sat playing his guitar that morning in front of his house. According to the plaintiff, the two attackers had walked past him and made some deprecating comments concerning his musical ability; words were then exchanged leading to the landing of several blows. The notary took down the sworn but unsigned statement of the complainant and then transcribed the testimony of several other witnesses who had been brought by the victim to aid him in establishing the facts of the case. It was evident from the testimony that the victim knew his attackers intimately and that the episode in question had probably occurred in slightly different form several times before.

The notary then proceeded to the office of the local constable who read the statements (or had them read to him) and announced that an official indictment had been opened against the two alleged attackers. This announcement was transcribed by the notary and put alongside the earlier statements. On 27 December the village doctor was questioned by the constable and stated that an examination of the defendant revealed a large bruise on one hand and a cut on the other, clear evidence of some recent altercation. This statement was then added to the dossier of the notary who again announced the preparation of an indictment and the preparation of a file to present before the magistrate in Toledo. It is important to note that the plaintiff was given an opportunity to withdraw his complaint every time that the local constable announced a continuation of the case. Yet in this particular incident the victim chose to continue the proceedings against his adversaries.

On 31 December the entire dossier was presented to the magistrate in Toledo by the local constable from Los Yebenes. The magistrate, called the *Fiel de Juzgado*, was a member of the city council chosen by his peers to serve in his judicial capacity for a term of one year. The post could be quite lucrative because the magistrate collected one-third of all fines assessed in criminal cases. Since the court probably read between 800 and 1,000 cases per year, this could amount to a very satisfactory emolument. Moreover it was an incentive to render a verdict in as many cases as possible, and we shall see below how this system could work in favour of both the plaintiff and defendant. It should also be noted that the *Fiel* was always a member of the lesser urban nobility (*regidor*), though he had no special training either in jurisprudence or any other aspect of the criminal system. Rather than representing the law in any impartial manner, the *Fiel* represented authority and thus rendered his decisions from that latter perspective rather than relying upon any strict attention to legal or judicial norms.

The magistrate held a first reading of the case and, on the basis of the written statements, instructed the constable to return to the village, arrest the individuals named as the defendants, sequester their personal possessions in lieu of bail, bring them to the city jail, and return the dossier for a second reading to the court. Upon returning to Los Yebenes the constable announced the decision of the magistrate and then proceeded to carry out his instructions. At this time the plaintiff was given another opportunity to withdraw his complaint, but again refused to do so. Consequently the two defendants were placed under detention in the settlement and their personal possessions (furniture, clothing) were seized and inventoried according to the quality and value of each item. If the defendant were later to escape from jail, as frequently happened, or fail to carry out any orders of the court, his possessions would be put up for auction in the village and the proceeds would pay the costs of his incarceration plus the salaries of the judicial officials.

On 2 January the constable informed the notary that all the orders of the court had been carried out. The two men were under arrest and their goods under the possession of the village authorities. Moreover the actions of the court in this case had been broadcast throughout the settlement by the *pregonero*, a town crier who walked from corner to corner and shouted out the news. In a village of no more than 400 households, this was a certain means of informing the entire population about the particular incident. The constable was legally required to inform the local population about his activities in this manner; thus the justice system as it operated on the local level was a perfect method for spreading the news of a particular incident throughout the entire village community. In many respects this was the most significant aspect of the procedure because the plaintiff could publicise his grievances and recapture any sense of lost honour or prestige.

On 11 January the process took a different course. The plaintiff announced that he was willing to settle the issue if the defendants would confess their crime and take full responsibility for the incident. The village doctor was again consulted and declared that the wounds of the plaintiff had healed satisfactorily, and that he had no further concern with the issue. At this point the record becomes somewhat unclear. The next entry dates from 22 February and is a statement by the *Fiel* in Toledo to the effect that the defendants had confessed their guilt in the attack upon Juan de Pedro Alameda, and that the court was ready to pronounce sentence in the case. There is no statement regarding where the two defendants spent the period from 2 January when they were incarcerated in Los Yebenes until 22 February when the case was finally settled. Quite possibly they were freed on bail in the settlement, since the local jail was only a make-shift operation and the jail in Toledo was reserved for persons charged with more serious crimes.

The text of the sentence makes clear that both the plaintiff and the defendants were consulted prior to the disposition of the case. The magistrate fined both men a minor sum (the equivalent of two days' wages for a rural labourer) which could be paid in full at a later date. At the same time the defendants swore an oath to cease any further injurious contact with the plaintiff. The magistrate inserted a statement in the sentence to the effect that failure to abide by the oath (known as *amistades*), might result in more severe penalties in the future. The case was then declared closed, with the dossier containing a final statement by the village constable providing that the decision of the court would again be broadcast throughout the entire village.

The case was significant because the plaintiff actually pushed the procedure through to a formal sentence. In a majority of criminal cases from this region the plaintiff dropped the original charge at some point in the proceeding, and allowed the defendant to plead to a lesser charge that resulted in a fine covering court costs rather than a stiffer penalty resulting from an actual sentence. Once a formal procedure was initiated, everyone in the judicial bureaucracy had a vested interest in arriving at some conclusion that allowed the magistrate to assess at least a small fine to cover judicial costs. Yet there was very little incentive to prosecute an offence to its conclusion, especially in cases of crimes against persons, and the plaintiff was given frequent opportunities to request an early termination of the case. At the same time the defendant was constantly reminded that a confession would not only terminate the case sooner but would result in an exceedingly light sentence, especially when compared to the penalties meted out to those who obstinately refused to admit their guilt.

It should also be noted that the entire procedure took place outside the courtroom. The magistrate in Toledo never saw either the plaintiff or the defendant, even if the latter was lodged in the jail that was located only several hundred metres from the courtroom itself. Yet it did not necessarily result in any flagrant miscarriages of justice and was probably no more arbitrary a system than trial proceedings carried on in open court. It is important to stress the extent to which a manipulative, private system invited great numbers of the most petty denunciations. Most of the crimes that were reported in private judicial systems would never have been brought up for judgement in a public court. Consequently there was no necessity to invest great time or money verifying the truth or falsity of a claim; the plaintiff in most cases was not so much interested in a guilty verdict as he was interested in avenging his sense of loss.

This last point is clearly the most important element in understanding the functioning of private criminal justice systems. The system rested upon the necessity to compensate the victim rather than punish the criminal. In fact the latter element was really incidental to the nature of the system even in cases of serious crime. At the same time the system had to adhere to the requirements of a bureaucratised, judicial structure in which all of the functionaries had a vested interest in justifying the necessity of their jobs. This meant that every crime had to be settled in the most efficient manner possible. Here again the question of punishment was far from an important priority. Court costs and salaries had to be met in some fashion and legalities would be observed insofar as these ends were attained.

The true place of punishment in a private system can be gauged more accurately with reference to the typical punishments employed. The basic form of punishment in all private systems was the fine, usually assessed even when the defendant was found innocent of some of the charges placed against him. Monetary fines were perfectly suited for punishments involving the upper classes, and had in fact evolved in response to the demand of the feudal aristocracy to formulate penalties that would allow them to escape corporal punishments. Yet the system of monetary fines did not work so well in a general sense, because the lower classes simply could not afford to pay them. Consequently other types of punishment had to be developed in order to retain the usefulness of the criminal justice system for all groups in feudal society.

The second most frequent type of punishment employed in the early period was banishment from the particular locale. A sentence of exile was a very severe penalty, because it meant that the individual had to find a place as a stranger in a society that placed the highest premium upon familiarity. On some occasions, banishment was equivalent to life imprisonment, because the unlucky culprit might then be arrested as a vagrant and sent to the galleys or perhaps even a worse fate. In the rural milieu, forced exile was usually reserved for those crimes in which the criminal posed a threat to the welfare of the community, for vagrants or paupers without homes, prostitutes, incorrigibles and indeed anyone whose normal course of behaviour might prove injurious to the delicate social fabric that held the local community together. The sentence of banishment was another indication of the extent to which feudal society was based upon localism and permanence of domicile within a particular group. It was also a penalty that required the cooperation of the entire community in order that it be carried out effectively, since a ban of exile would be broken if a member of the community spied the culprit lurking about the local settlement.

There were other types of punishment during the Middle Ages, although much less common than either fines or banishments. Prisons were not unknown and incarceration was a fairly common form of punishment even for such minor offences as petty larceny. But lengthy prison sentences were never a regular aspect of medieval punishment and the longest terms prescribed in medieval law codes were less than five years. In most cases, such as the one detailed above, detention was a trial procedure, but even here it was rare that a prisoner languished in jail for more than several months.[5] By the fourteenth century in England all jailed prisoners had to be delivered to court every six months. Part of the reason for brief prison stays lay in the structure and administration of medieval prisons. The warden of the prison often owned the premises, or rented them for the purpose of running a penal institution. In either case the prison was expected to show a profit, and prisoners required, if possible, to pay the costs of their own incarceration. Naturally most prisoners paid less as their stay behind bars lengthened, and there was thus an incentive to change the composition of the prison population as frequently as possible. As a result, although prison conditions were usually appallingly bad, sentences were usually quite brief and hence fairly mild.

There was also little resort to corporal punishment at the beginning of the early modern period, except for the use of stocks and the pillory. Both devices were set up in public, and the victim could be displayed for ridicule and abuse by other members of the community. Stocks were often used to punish crimes of a general nature, such as unscrupulous business methods. In this case, as in other forms of punishment, the primary motivation was to avenge the sense of loss felt by the community rather than inflict some serious punishment upon the offender. Like the town crier (*pregonero*) in the Spanish village, the use of stocks on an English village common alerted the entire community to the unsavoury activities of a particular individual. Stocks could also be used to keep a runaway servant in view until he was identified and word sent back to his master. Once again the emphasis in punishment was on the maintenance of traditional social relations, rather than on the punishment of a culprit *per se*.

Although corporal punishments, such as branding and whipping, were quite rare during this period, executions were not unknown. Except in cases of treason, execution was usually by hanging. Theoretically capital punishment could be prescribed in any felony case, including larceny and felonious assault. However the number of felony convictions always exceeded by far the number of capital sentences, and the number of persons condemned to death was always far greater than the number of actual executions. Medieval court rolls from English counties in the period 1250–1450 suggest that less than half all felony convictions resulted in a sentence other than banishment, and perhaps one in ten sentences included a decree of execution. Moreover few of those latter individuals were ever brought before the executioner.

There were several reasons for this wide discrepancy

between statutory and actual punishment. First, local courts were loath to pass a severe sentence upon a defendant who was known in the community and probably on familiar terms with members of the judicial staff themselves. Second, medieval law allowed mitigating circumstances, such as illness, poverty or insanity, to be taken into account in sentencing a defendant. Finally, pardons were not only common in capital crimes but were a convenient pretext for increasing the amount of monetary assessment in lieu of a decree of execution. Certain individuals moreover were virtually guaranteed the possibility of a pardon, regardless of the offence for which they had been found guilty. Faithful service in the king's army was the basis for a pardon and this arrangement had an obvious social logic behind it. Soldiers returning from long campaigns were often unable to fit back into civilian life and their military experiences made criminal activity a natural alternative. A pardon for crimes committed under these circumstances was a tacit recognition of the sacrifices made by the soldier in acquitting himself with honour fighting for his king.

From every perspective the definition of crime and the treatment of criminals at the beginning of the early modern period reflected the basic social structure of the feudal age. Crime was considered a private affair, closely related to the extreme bonds of friendship, kinship and status that dominated medieval social relations. Crime was also considered to be an affair among equals, and this conception reflected the extent to which the feudal world still rested upon an equal communality of work and experiences. The most serious crimes were those that threatened to upset the delicate social balance of the community; anything else could be settled in a private manner.

The social structure of the medieval world also shaped the manner in which crime was controlled. The community bore full responsibility for its prevention, as well as for insuring that sentences were carried out to their full extent. Punishment likewise served social ends: it enabled an individual to avenge his sense of loss and it enabled the community to identify troublesome individuals in its midst. The criminal justice system allowed for personal manipulation of the system because crime was personal; it was usually the act of one person against someone with whom he was previously acquainted. It could hardly have been otherwise in a community where literally every individual had some sort of social or familial relationship with everyone else. Thus in the early period punishment fit crime, just as crime fit the society in which it was committed. We shall now see how society, crime and punishment began to change.

CHAPTER 3
EUROPE AND EUROPEAN CRIME BEGIN TO CHANGE

By the middle of the fifteenth century, at a time when European society had fully recovered from the long-term effects of the Black Plague, certain social and economic developments were set in motion. These developments would eventually transform the entire shape of European society, as well as change the whole nature of crime. The most important development in this respect was the enormous change in the demographic situation that began to occur sometime after 1450. This would result in the population of Europe increasing by more than half from that date up to the end of the sixteenth century. This increase in population was most noticeable in the cities, which in some places grew three times as fast as the general increase in population. Not only did Europe experience a sort of demographic revolution (although population growth after 1750 would be much more sustained), but there was also a vast movement of population from one place to another. It was this latter aspect of the demographic situation – mobility – that most clearly contrasted with the demographic experience of the medieval period. For while the population of Europe had always undergone cyclical variations over time, there had never been such a sustained, upward movement of population coupled with the mobility of so many persons of every social class. In England, for example, it has been estimated that by 1640 only 15 per cent of the rural population was living in the same village as their ancestors had been a century before.

The greatest difference occurred in urban centres, where whole new neighbourhoods came into existence to accommodate the vast new urban population, most of it recently arrived in the larger towns. It is now becoming clear that not only was the European population much more mobile during this period but elements of it were travelling far greater distances than ever before. Whereas medieval towns rarely attracted immigrants or travellers from beyond the limits of the region, immigration from one area to another now became national in scope. In Madrid, a city that experienced a phenomenal population growth in the last part of the sixteenth century, whole neighbourhoods developed around populations that had come from specific, far-flung regions in Spain; there was a *barrio* (quarter) for Basque immigrants, another area of the town was settled only by Galicians, and a third of the city was literally reserved for immigrants from Leon. The European city was no longer a small, tightly-knit community in which most people had an identifiable social or economic rank. It was being transformed into an enormous agglomeration that contained a very diverse population. By the end of the sixteenth century a literary genre that praised rustic life in reaction to these unparalleled and uncontrolled urban developments had sprung up throughout Europe. Middleton in England and Lope de Vega in Spain both captured in their dramas the drift of events in the urban environment as economic activities, social values and cultural ideals all underwent a dramatic transformation.

This demographic change, although perhaps operating primarily for natural, biological reasons, was also clearly related to fundamental developments in the European economy. These developments encompassed two general elements: the emergence of an international economy geared to mass commodity trade, and the transformation of the rural economy away from a subsistence base toward a mixed economy supporting both grain production and the production of raw industrial commodities. Linking the commercial and rural sectors, first in England and later in the Low Countries, Italy and France, was the textile industry with the beginnings of modern craft production and the substitution of cheap woollens for traditional, luxury fabrics. Alongside these basic developments arose a number of secondary factors that also played an important role in the economic growth of western Europe: the extension of credit, improvements in transportation, the spread of education and the elaboration of new technologies. The history of this economic growth is too well known to necessitate further discussion here. Our interest is to demonstrate how these new social and economic developments affected the profile of European crime.

Let us look first at how new types of social alignment emerged in the rural sector in response to economic developments of the early modern period. Despite differences of historical opinion it is now clear that some widening occurred in the gap between rich and poor peasants over the course of the sixteenth century. Whether or not a new class of yeomen farmers emerged only as a result of the enclosures is quite apart from the fact that, by the end, of the Elizabethan period, the groundwork had been laid for a new social structure in the countryside. In many rural areas a majority of the population had become largely detached from the land and villages now contained a rural proletariat alongside the traditional agricultural labour force. R. H. Tawney once showed that, of the active population in the Midlands in 1604, only 46 per cent were engaged in agricultural tasks, while a majority of the workforce were engaged in such non-agricultural activities as textiles, leather and clothing manufacture, mining, construction and food supply.[1] Although changes were initially most obvious in England they occurred in other European countries as well. The emergence of the *labrador* class in backward Spain exemplified the trend toward social polarisation in the countryside.

The embryonic industrialisation of the rural zone was paralleled by a growing commercialisation of the countryside as peasant artisans and yeomen found that selling goods at regional markets allowed them to buy a wide range of manufactured articles. Trade fairs flourished at the local level; travelling merchants and tradesmen were now common in every country hamlet. At the same time urban entrepreneurs flooded the rural areas with primary materials, eagerly utilising rural labour to offset the high costs of production in towns still controlled by the old guilds.

We must be careful, however, not to overstate the extent of the European economic advance between the mid-fifteenth century and the close of the sixteenth century. Even at the end of the seventeenth century the basic production of the European economy still rested upon primary commodities harvested from the land. Yet it was also the case that the economic changes of the period 1450–1700 were sufficient in scope to produce a social structure in the countryside that had never previously existed. The rural population was now much more diverse, mobile, and fragmented than under the feudal regime. That part of the population whose labour linked the urban and rural sectors had grown enormously, reflecting the great increase in economic relations between the two sectors. Although the countryside was still far from modern, the last vestiges of medieval cohesion and stability had been shattered beyond repair.

Social changes in the cities of Europe were likewise quite extensive and resulted in the irreversible transformation of urban society. The beginnings of modern textile production brought about the appearance of the workshop and the movement of industrial labour from the home. At the same time textiles and related trades developed to such an extent that every large city would soon contain, in embryo, the makings of a true, working-class population. Over time a larger proportion of the workforce would become engaged in various types of labour where wages, rather than working conditions, were the primary attraction to the working masses.

Perhaps the greatest changes occurred in the areas of commerce and trade, for it was here that economic activity in the sixteenth and seventeenth centuries was most intense. Trade was not only a function of international commercial relations but was founded much more upon the exchange of raw and finished materials between the cities and their rural hinterlands. The urban population was now so great and their needs for foodstuffs so extensive that a national workforce developed to supply these goods on a daily basis. The best example of this state of affairs was London which, by the seventeenth century, was drawing foodstuffs from as far away as Wales and the Scottish Highlands. At the north of the city whole areas were turned into depots and markets where produce, meat and other commodities were unloaded, sold and sent to retail outlets throughout the metropolis. At the southern end were the wharves with their own army of workmen employed in loading ships and other activities connected with overseas trade. London shipping was so widespread by the seventeenth century that the city contained many neighbourhoods settled almost exclusively by foreigners who had come to the town in order to direct overseas trade back to their countries of origin. Some of these groups, like the Venetians, were large enough to support their own private cemeteries.

London was certainly not the only large metropolis to undergo these extensive changes. The Paris market rivalled that of London in the amount of commodities that arrived daily. Moreover the area from which these products were drawn was also quite extensive. By the seventeenth century farms within a radius of nearly 100 kilometres were producing food for the Paris market and a large network of local roads had been developed around the city for the purpose of effecting transit from outlying rural zones. Other cities also witnessed the development of social and economic activities on a scale never previously imagined. Seville, which had nearly tripled in size during the sixteenth century, now held a population of great diversity as businessmen and merchants from all over Europe scrambled to share in the profits of New World voyages. Likewise the Italian ports of Genoa and Venice had become entrepôts in the modern sense of the term.

As in the countryside the results of this economic transformation could be seen in the changes in the lives of both the rich and the poor. By the middle of the seventeenth century most European cities contained a commercial/industrial bourgeoisie whose wealth and power would soon pose a serious challenge to the old aristocratic élite. This new middle-class had impinged also upon the domain of the aristocracy in a much more fundamental manner: as a result of debt contracts or outright purchase they had come to control large amounts of rural real estate that could be used as an investment as well as a means for attaining and consolidating social position. At the same time there was a significant change in the size and makeup of the urban lower classes. Their numbers increased tremendously, in part a reflection of the magnetic effects of urban industrialisation, in part due to the transformation of the rural sector. We have not yet arrived at the point when urban slums would become the overwhelming environment for a majority of the city population. That development would only occur alongside the growth of the factory system at the end of the eighteenth century. Nonetheless an urban proletariat was well on its way to formation at least a century before that time.

The character of work was also beginning to change. Although a majority of the working poor in the cities remained grouped within the service sector, moving between the needs of the mercantile and industrial complexes, new differences could now be discerned. As the economy became more specialised the working population began to divide into a number of definite occupational groups. Over time there would be less mobility between various occupations and gradually a distinction developed between the working and the non-working poor. At the same time there was a marked erosion of the status and position of the skilled worker; some of them would be siphoned off into the lower ranks of the mercantile class but many more would find their circumstances more closely resembling that of semi-skilled workers. These developments would all take time and even by the end of the seventeenth century the profile of the urban workforce would still have a clear, pre-modern stamp. Yet the drift of events was unmistakably clear. In both the urban and rural sectors, economic development had promoted both economic and social polarisation. The gap between the rich and the poor had grown wider in terms of living standards, economic activities and social values.

The development of a new working population was paralleled by the emergence of a new labouring cycle which would have an enormous impact upon the type and extent of crime during this period. Just as the mobility of population in the early modern period could be contrasted with the immobility of the medieval period, so labour in the later era also took on a more transient nature. The increase in trade and commerce, particularly the movement of grains and other primary commodities within each region, meant that a great number of persons engaged in this trade were now moving from place to place on a regular basis. This constant movement of working persons, often confused with the travels of beggars and tramps, was augmented by the large number of local tradesmen, merchants and peasant entrepreneurs who plied their wares or the goods of others in villages and at local fairs. As the general population increased and moved, it necessitated a large-scale rebuilding of homes and dwellings throughout Europe. England in the sixteenth century experienced what one scholar has called 'a housing revolution',[2] and this gave rise to an impressive construction industry whose work-force, then as now, had to move from place to place in order to continue their labour.

The mobility of non-agricultural labour had its counterpart in an increase in the seasonality of many labouring activities. In place of the regular harvest cycle that governed the rhythm of both urban and rural economic activities, many workers now faced the uncertain industrial cycle of the early modern period. This cycle was usually characterised by a constant series of immediate booms and slumps that wreaked social havoc upon the working population. Inclement weather, delays in securing raw materials, market crises and credit liquidations all combined to produce sharp and unanticipated declines in industrial production. The fact that many textile producers farmed out their goods to the rural sector meant that any trade or commercial crisis in the cities would have grave repercussions throughout every level of society. Since population increase regularly outpaced productive capacity both in industry and agriculture there was little possibility that a slump in one sector could be alleviated by shifting a portion of the workforce into the other. Rather, such events resulted in unemployment and social dislocation as near-constant factors in the lives of the working population.

Bearing all this in mind, let us examine the profile of crime in the rural sector during this period. The quantitative evidence that we possess shows a marked increase in all types of reported crime during the period 1500–1700 and particularly after the latter half of the sixteenth century. Some of the increase in certain types of crime was no doubt attributable to population growth, but crime levels rose at a much faster pace than the overall increase in population. This was probably due to a general deterioration in the living standards of the rural masses. Although there was never an exact correlation between short-term shifts in living standards (as measured by real wages) and criminality, there was a rough coincidence of the two trends over time. Thus in villages in the central Castilian plateau, crime levels increased by between 200 per cent and 300 per cent over the period 1575–1630 while real wages declined by more than one-third. In rural England specific years of poor harvests did not yield particularly high crime levels, but on an overall basis lower harvest levels were paralleled by significant increases in the amount of crime.

The class nature of criminal activity in the rural sector was a further confirmation of the social context in which crime was now beginning to occur. In the county of Essex, where nearly 70 per cent of all felonies were various types of larceny, at least half the felons were classified as labourers, with yeomen and husbandmen appearing as defendants in fewer than one-fifth of all indictments. In the Spanish province of Toledo, larceny was not quite as prevalent as in rural Essex, but defendants in those cases came almost exclusively from the lowest ranks of village society. Moreover this widespread incidence of lower-class theft was not the work of a small segment of the poor population. Rather it was an activity that embraced the energies of a large proportion of the village poor. In rural Essex nearly 85 per cent of all defendants in felony cases had never previously appeared before the magistrate, and only 4 per cent of all felons had been in court as felons before. In Spanish settlements, repeat offenders were so rare as to be statistically negligible; in one village more than 80 different persons were indicted for larceny over the course of a year out of a population of no more than 400 families. This lack of repeated offenders among the criminal population could not be blamed upon the severity of punishment, because defendants in both areas were rarely sentenced to long-term banishments or serious corporal penalties. Rather it reflected the fact that theft had become ubiquitous among the lower classes of the countryside.

It has been possible to recover a good deal of statistical evidence on rural crime during the sixteenth and seventeenth century. The data presented here come from two quite disparate regions: the Montes de Toledo in Spain

and the rural portion of the English county of Essex.³
The villages of the Montes de Toledo in the province of
Toledo were some of the most isolated and backward in
all western Europe. They were located in an environment that could only sustain a minimal subsistence
economy and they had only the most limited contacts
with nearby urban centres. Moreover most of the Montes
settlements were quite small, ranging from 700 families
down to hamlets of less than 75 households. Yet despite
the general backwardness of the area, the economic and
social developments of sixteenth-century Spain had
affected even this zone. Population had more than
doubled between 1550 and 1600 and some of the larger
villages had witnessed the faint beginnings of artisan and
craft activities in response to demand from the urban
markets of Toledo and Talavera de la Reina. The data on
crime cover the period 1585–1630, with the bulk of it
occurring during the last two decades of that period,
when villages experienced a severe demographic and
economic crisis.

Crime in the Montes could be divided roughly into
attacks on persons and attacks on property. Within each
category there were many sub-categories; thus crimes of
violence included assault, aggravated assault, rape, libel,
slander, disturbing the peace and riot. Crimes against
property included theft, burglary, criminal trespass, fraud
and illegal business activities. Together these two categories of crime accounted for more than 75 per cent of
all the criminal indictments between 1585 and 1630. Of
that total there were about an equal proportion of violent
crimes and crimes against property. Yet the proportions
of crimes in each settlement tended to vary according to
the size and wealth of the particular village. In the largest
village, Los Yebenes, violent crime accounted for 47 per

cent of all indictable offences, while crimes against property constituted only about 30 per cent of all reported crime. In another large settlement, Ventas, violent crime represented 44 per cent of all reported criminal incidents and crimes against property 33 per cent of all reported crime. In the smaller settlements however this profile was reversed. The tiny village of San Pablo, containing only about 125 families in 1625, witnessed a 50 per cent rate of crimes against property while recording only a 35 per cent rate of personal violence. Another small village, Navahermosa, also had a 50 per cent rate of crimes against property with a slightly lower (33 per cent) rate of crimes against persons.

The proportion of violent crime to crimes against property was not so much an index of the size of the settlement as it reflected the overall wealth of the local population. Yet the prosperity of the village was also closely tied to its size. The per capita wealth of village residents in Yebenes, the largest settlement, was twice that of the residents of a medium-sized village like Ventas and more than three times greater than levels of per capita wealth in the smallest settlements. Therefore crimes against property were a clear reflection of the social situation in each settlement. Those villages in which a great number of persons were poor experienced an extremely high rate of larceny while those villages with a greater degree of economic development tended to have less activity in the area of crimes against property.

In rural Essex the situation was somewhat different. This was not a backward and remote area like the Montes de Toledo. On the contrary, Essex was a primary area of production for the London market. It possessed a good deal of cottage industry and its main artery, the Colchester-London road, was usually crowded with traffic moving between the province and the urban metropolis on the Thames. The evidence for Essex shows a preponderance of robbery, burglary and theft during the second half of the sixteenth century. In fact, from 1559 to 1603, crimes against property appear to have accounted for more than 90 per cent of all reported felonies. Over the course of the period moreover the proportion of felony larcenies actually increased from about 85 per cent to 95 per cent. This increase occurred at the same time that the crime rate apparently doubled while population probably increased by about one-third.

Obviously larceny had become the single most important type of crime in rural Europe. Yet while it had always been the most prevalent type of criminal activity its character was beginning to change in certain crucial respects during this period. As opposed to earlier times, when rural thieves concentrated almost exclusively upon taking subsistence items, larceny now included the theft of luxury items and other articles whose value could only be realised through some sort of exchange. Rural thieves no longer took only those items that they or their associates could immediately consume; objects of material value were included in criminal thefts as well. Rural larceny was still overwhelmingly tied to the taking of items of limited value that could be consumed within the immediate circle around the thief. But now there was a new element to be added to the profile of rural criminality.

The appearance of luxury goods as objects of theft was indicative of a number of important social changes in the structure of rural society. The existence of luxury items in the rural milieu was a reflection of the growth of the yeoman class and its attempts to imitate the urban, petty bourgeoisie in the acquisition and exhibition of nonessential items. The theft of these items was clearly related to the ability of the rural thief to maintain communication with the urban centre, and this demonstrated the extent to which the rural hamlet was connected to a regular network of communication and trade. It was no longer unusual for many members of the local settlement to journey to the city on a regular basis, and this allowed for the transportation of contraband items out of the settlement without arousing any suspicion. In Spain, for example, peasants living along the edge of the Gaudarrama mountains made a goodly and illegal living by stealing wood out of seigneurial domains and carting it nearly sixty kilometres to be sold at Madrid. The true nature of their activities was disguised by the fact that legal carting of wood from this region to the capital city was a constant activity.

The result of this ability to utilise outside channels of communication lay in the fact that larceny was no longer an intra-class activity in the rural zone. In fact a growing social distinction emerged between the social class of the criminal as opposed to that of his victim. Poor peasants no longer stole only from their neighbours but began taking items from wealthier village residents as well. Crime in rural Europe was moving away from its intra-class character and was beginning to develop as an aspect of inter-class conflict. This development related both to the worsening condition of the lower classes, as well as to changes in the social composition of rural society.

Another type of criminality that had existed since the Middle Ages was banditry, and its changing character during the early modern period is an important clue to understanding the social effects of the transformation to modern life. The use of the word 'bandit' was itself indicative of the modern age; it did not exist in English usage until the end of the sixteenth century, and then had been derived from Elizabethan descriptions of highway men operating along the Appenine range in central Italy. Previously these individuals had been called 'outlaws', but this expression denoted a much different set of circumstances and motives. The term literally meant to be 'outside the law', indicating both a legal and social reality of the Middle Ages. Since law operated within a local jurisdiction, lawbreakers could easily be banished beyond the geographical limits of that particular system or could escape the law by moving beyond its legal boundaries. In many cases the latter motive explained the existence of outlaws who were persons of high social standing. Sometimes members of the gentry were involved in blood feuds and became outlaws until their legal and social situations were resolved.

In the sixteenth century, when the outlaw was replaced by the bandit, this transformation indicated the existence of a legal system that no longer tolerated self-exile. The bandit did not exist beyond the law because national jurisdictions were replacing the older, more localised systems. Bandits simply existed beyond the momentary inability of the legal authorities to track them down, despite the fact that mounted police often went to great lengths to protect important highways. By the seventeenth century most national thoroughfares in Europe were regularly patrolled and bandits could operate successfully only in remote areas where they would not long survive, or along unimportant political frontiers where precise national jurisdictions had never been settled.

At the same time the social character of bandit gangs began to change; they were no longer comprised of members of the gentry but were now composed almost exclusively of the poor. Quite frequently bandit gangs included many habitual felons who had no choice but to resort to banditry, since the punishment from which they were escaping would be severe. It should also be noted that although bandit gangs usually operated in remote mountain zones, their numbers often included former urban residents who had been forced out of the city by economic circumstances. Bandit gangs in the mountains of Catalonia, according to Vilar, contained artisans and other urban craftsmen whom one would not ordinarily expect to find amidst this particular population.[4] But this was simply another reflection of the profound social changes that were occurring in the general population during the early stages of the transition.

Urban criminality during this period was also a continuation of some of the earlier patterns, modified as time went on by the changing social situation. City crime still primarily took the form of larceny though this general category was now divided into several new types. For one thing the sixteenth and seventeenth centuries saw the appearance of the definitive urban crime – mugging – in all its variations. For the first time city streets were thought to be unsafe, particularly after nightfall. Internal security could no longer be guaranteed by closing the gates of the town in the evening and only admitting local residents thereafter. Now the city population contained a criminal element that operated at all hours within the confines of the urban milieu. The security of the medieval urban centre no longer existed.

Urban larceny during this period also began to exhibit another very modern variation, namely fraud and various types of confidence games. A new criminal ethos developed around the swindle: it became the chief means of stealing items of great value without actually effecting an illegal entry. The swindle was the antithesis of the honest business deal, although infinite business deals had spawned the new urban mess that everyone tolerated and nobody condoned. An entire literary genre known as the picaresque grew up around this activity. The first works appeared in Spain, notably *Lazarillo de Tormes* and *Guzmán de Alfarache*. These novels set the tone and structure of the picaresque genre, both in terms of the moral symbolism of the work as well as the essential elements of the plot. By the seventeenth century, the picaresque novel began to fade in Spain, with the last important work, *Estebanillo González*, appearing in 1646. However, the genre then emerged in Germany, notably in *Der abenteuerliche Simplicissimus* (*The Adventurous Simplicissimus*), written by Jacob von Grimmelshausen in 1668. By this time imitations of the picaresque novel were appearing in England, though the originality of the English picaresque tradition would be signalled by the publication of *Moll Flanders* in 1722.

In its early form the picaresque novel celebrated the adventures of the urban rogue, or *pícaro*, his attempt to avoid honest work and the possibilities offered by the urban environment for all sorts of knavery. There is no doubt that many elements of the picaresque novel can best be explained with reference to earlier literary traditions, and the relationship between this particular literary genre and European cultural traditions at that time. But the picaresque was also *real*. It was a poignant comment upon a state of affairs that had developed in European society and in European cities as they emerged from the medieval age. This new criminal environment is captured brilliantly in the pages of Cervantes' *Rinconete and Cortadillo*, where the two young thieves are by stages initiated into a criminal existence controlled by the crime entrepreneur Monipodio who operated out of the jail in Seville.

Urban criminality during this period was also characterised by the existence of a true underworld, complete with its haunts and special neighbourhoods. In some of these places the population was even divided according to the criminal speciality of the inhabitants. In Madrid the Lavapies section was notorious in this respect, containing all manner of ruffians, thieves and street criminals. Every type of stolen goods could be acquired (and even ordered) at the proper price. Seville's criminal population frequented a large courtyard which was located alongside the cathedral and featured an all-night restaurant along with many other diversions. The densest criminal area in Paris, the *cour des miracles* near the Porte St.-Denis, was so extensive that it remained impregnable to official control until it was invaded and destroyed by a regular army detachment in 1667.

The existence of such neighbourhoods was partially the result of a public policy that tolerated 'red-light' districts in every large town. Nobody has yet studied the quasi-legal relationships that existed between municipal authorities and brothel-masters or other vice entrepreneurs in urban centres. Yet the existence of vice neighbourhoods institutionalised illicit sexual activities and brought about the emergence of sex as another aspect of the urban service economy. Like every other marginal form of labour, prostitution and related vices employed large numbers of transients and particularly homeless women who had the greatest difficulty finding other means of subsistence. The prostitute population of many cities was quite large, although it was usually far underrepresented in official surveys conducted by municipal authorities. In Rome during the sixteenth century there may have been as many as 25,000 prostitutes out of a population of about 100,000. This figure may be somewhat high though it is known that Pius V failed in his attempt to expel the prostitutes from Rome in 1566 because of the dire effects that were forecast for the Roman economy. Municipal governments were aware of the lucrative aspects of the vice trade in other areas as well. The market town of Medina del Campo in northern Spain established municipal brothels and made a healthy profit from their business. In Toledo the town council appropriated the necessary funds to rebuild the brothel located outside the Bisagra gate after it had burned to the ground in 1624.

The toleration of these sorts of criminal activities was in part a result of fiscal expediency and in part an element of the necessity to control these activities in a legal form in order to discourage their spread. But it also reflected the recognition that new demands for labour produced certain new or expanded forms of lawlessness that could not be erased so long as the need for labour itself existed. If in some instances the alternative to providing the rich with labour was providing the wealthy classes with sexual pleasure, then this was all the more reason to tolerate such activities.

CHAPTER 4

EUROPE REACTS TO THE NEW CRIME

During the sixteenth and seventeenth centuries, modern systems of criminal justice and criminal punishment began to emerge in Europe. The methods of dealing with crime were still far removed from what they would be in the nineteenth century. But they were perhaps even further removed from their feudal predecessors. For it was during this period that criminal justice would make the crucial transition from the private to the public domain. This transformation was not only the result of certain political developments but also reflected the reaction of society to some new social factors that had developed as well.

For the first time since the fall of Rome the problem of social unrest in Europe had begun to assume significant dimensions. There had been many times during the Middle Ages when mass riots or rebellions had threatened the general welfare; indeed wholesale uprisings had occurred with great frequency, particularly during the fourteenth century. But that feature was quite distinct from the emergence of a large, lower class for which petty crime directed at the upper classes became a basic way of life. It was the class character of this crime that made it so different from earlier criminality, and it was the class character of crime that threatened the social order in a much more fundamental manner.

This new crime could not be controlled simply by

amplifying medieval criminal procedures to cover the increased incidence of illegal activities. For one thing methods for controlling crime in the medieval period had been predicated upon the existence of a small population living in a compact area and isolated from other populations. But in general these conditions no longer existed and the social basis of the new criminality reflected the extent to which conditions had changed. Furthermore the medieval criminal justice system had been based upon a politically localised and fragmented structure that was rapidly being displaced by the growth of the national state: this institution would ultimately refashion every part of the legal system to meet its own ends. In order to control the new crime, a system would have to be devised that transformed criminal justice from a private matter involving particular individuals into a public matter involving anonymous individuals and the state. This was more in keeping with a political system that rested upon sovereign rather than personal authority. It was also more suited to a pattern of criminality that occurred increasingly within anonymous circumstances.

Two significant procedural changes of the sixteenth century were the emergence of a different method of prosecution and the promulgation of new criminal codes. These developments marked an important phase in the transition from private to public criminal systems and were clear evidence of the extent to which the national state was beginning to intervene actively in the administration of criminal justice throughout Europe. It was also a reflection of the extent to which the older systems were no longer applicable to the problems posed by early modern criminality. Prosecution could no longer be a local affair because crime was no longer localised. Criminal codes had to become more comprehensive because the societies governed by those codes were also evolving as national entities. Let us look first at the development of new prosecutorial techniques, exemplified most dramatically by the emergence of the Justice of the Peace in England.

It is generally believed that the task of apprehending criminals belonged in the medieval period to the sheriff and that his basic role was later superseded by the powers of the Justice of the Peace. To a certain extent this is true, but the appearance of the JP as the chief law enforcement officer of the Crown also resulted in certain important changes in the judicial system as a whole. For by the time that the JP emerged as the head of the criminal justice system in England an entirely new criminal procedure had evolved. The JP was a crucial figure in this process, not only because of his power to arrest, indict and grant bail, but for the role he came to play in the trial process. In the long run the maturation of the court system and the greater reliance upon the jury to decide matters of criminal justice would result in the JP's losing some of his earlier authority, further evidence of the extent to which the English judicial process had moved away from its medieval base. In other words the JP was himself a transitional figure whose activities would move English criminal procedure from the private to the public domain. This occurred in the following way.

During the Middle Ages the sheriff was the chief administrative officer of the local court system. In particular he collected indictments at the local level and delivered them to the king's justices. He also presided over the county court where minor claims of trespass and various lesser infractions involving personal services were settled. His most important task during the feudal period, however, was to organise and supervise the frank-pledge, an extraordinary procedural device that perfectly illustrates the personalised and localised nature of medieval criminal systems. Under the procedure known as frankpledge, every adult male was enrolled in a group of ten adults, called a tithing. The sheriff was required to maintain all tithings at their full number, and only members of the aristocracy and clergy were generally exempted from service. The appearance in court of any member of the tithing to answer a criminal charge had to be guaranteed by the other nine members of the group. If a suspect failed to appear in court at the appointed time a fine could be assessed against the tithing to which he belonged. Hence the tithing system encouraged cooperation among all members both in the prevention of crime and in the treatment of offenders.

The entire tithing procedure fell into disuse by the end of the Middle Ages. The rationale behind the tithing system had been the schedule of the eyre, or king's court, which was held only several times each year as the magistrates travelled throughout the realm. As the business of the royal bench increased, visiting court procedures became less frequent and the rationale for the tithing process likewise disappeared. At the same time the practice of tithing was predicated upon the existence of a small, stable population that was accustomed to perform many tasks in a communal manner, a practice which became less common as the Middle Ages wore on. Consequently, for both legal and social reasons, the criminal procedures in which the sheriff played a major role became less important, and the overall power of the office was diminished. The sheriff remained a functionary in the criminal justice system throughout the entire early modern period though the nature of that system changed drastically.

The office of the JP also dates back to the early Middle Ages in England, and many of the duties of the post were enunciated in statutes by the fourteenth century. However, in the fifteenth century, the Justices began to take on more responsibilities and assume new powers, largely owing to the growth in the power of the Monarchy as well as to the increasing importance of the Commons. In fact from the earliest times the Justices were representatives of royal authority and were drawn from the ranks of the same gentry and urban bourgeois classes that dominated the Commons during that period. Consequently the JP became an instrument through which national power could be exerted over traditional, local authority.

Initially the JP functioned as an investigator, checking the veracity of indictments and serving as the representative of the King and the Privy Council at various judicial functions. However the powers of the JP widened consistently over the course of the fourteenth and fifteenth centuries. A Justice could make summary arrests for a variety of offences, particularly crimes related to mob violence or mass unrest, and this also led to an eventual takeover of the bail system. Most importantly, by the end of the fifteenth century, the activity of the JPs in Quarter Sessions courts allowed them to move from a position of initiating procedure to determining the scope of courtroom activity and controlling the sentencing of offenders. Thus the JP took over the entire scope of criminal procedure, and in this development one finds the emergence of two legal procedures based upon an amalgamation of royal prerogative and Commons pressure: the use of common law and the increased reliance upon juries to settle criminal disputes. Both elements accentuated the shift from private to public law in early modern England, and followed directly from the increased importance of the Justices in the functioning of the criminal law system.

The greatest impact of the JPs on criminal procedure was felt in the sixteenth century when, paradoxically enough, their judicial roles were diminished while their statutory roles were increased. The later development came as the result of the promulgation of numerous acts establishing criminal penalties for various types of labour offences such as failing to report to work, breaking tools, recalcitrance and so forth. Labour statutes first appeared in the fourteenth century but increased greatly in number and severity of punishment over the next two hundred years. Their enactment reflected the dissolution of the feudal order and the consequent need to find new methods to discipline the servile population. These laws were also indicative of the new economic relations developing in early modern society and the social tensions that arose alongside these new relationships.

At first, labour laws were drawn up to cover such aspects of the situation as wage rates, working conditions and other non-criminal elements of the newly-evolving labour structure. In a labour market that was not yet capitalist but no longer feudal, statute replaced tradition, while legal compulsion regulated supply and demand. Criminal law was thus used to enforce a new set of social relations and the JPs would serve a critical function in the expediting of these new laws. Since these statutes were promulgated on a national basis it was logical that the Justices would be empowered to ensure that they were carried out. Consequently JPs were granted complete authority to oversee the application of labour codes and their powers were increasingly widened with the passage of various poor laws during the same period. The authority of the Justices was enormously strengthened by the enactment of the Statute of Labour in 1563. The promulgation of this measure, following the passage of the Statute of Alehouses in 1552, allowed the JPs to move to the centre of the criminal justice system. For these acts embraced a wide variety of social offences and the JP was given ultimate authority to see that the laws were obeyed. The changing character of crime had now been answered by a change in the criminal codes and, as crime was more frequently defined in social terms, this led to an increase in the authority of those responsible for maintaining social norms.

On the continent there was a similar development of a chief prosecuting officer, although without as wide a set of powers as those that had accrued to the Justices of the Peace. In France the prosecutorial activity became institutionalised in the office of the *procureur du roi*, who appeared in the late thirteenth century but assumed the great bulk of his powers several centuries thereafter. The *procureur* became the plaintiff in cases where there was no private initiator of a case. Later he became the prosecutor in every criminal proceeding even when there was a private complainant. The growth in the *procureur*'s authority resulted largely from the gradual disassociation of the medieval magistrates from criminal cases. As we shall see, many types of criminal cases in France were ultimately turned into civil actions and it was in these procedures that the judge retained his primary role. This left the field of criminal procedure open to the initiative of the *procureur du roi*.

The second important procedural development of the early modern period was the appearance of new criminal procedures. In England these codes were contained within the Marian statutes that appeared in 1554–55 during the reign of Queen Mary. In Germany the basic attempt to reform prosecutorial procedure was contained within the text of the *Carolina*, a statute enacted in its final form by the Reichstag in 1532. In France the attempt to produce a new model for prosecutorial behaviour was introduced in the Ordinance of Villers-Cotterets, promulgated in 1539. The coincidence of dates should not lull the reader into assuming that the methods adopted in one code were directly influenced by the others. Although it has often been thought that the Marian statutes represented the 'invasion' of continental ideas into English law, a thorough reading of the texts and an understanding of their procedural implications show that this was not the case. In fact the procedures embodied in these various codes would lead to very different courtroom policies in England as opposed to the continent. However in both cases it also resulted in the final triumph of public law, the disappearance of the last vestiges of private law, and the institutionalisation of modern criminal procedure. The appearance of these codes at the same time was less a reflection of statutory influence and more an indication of the relative development of new criminal problems that these codes sought to counteract.

The Marian statutes established the legal necessity to collect all the facts about a particular incident and present them in the form of a written dossier. This became another responsibility of the JPs, who were now required to develop a written record of the case based upon an examination of witnesses and a conscientious recording of their unsworn statements. This evidence would not be submitted to the court but would aid the Justice in presenting oral, sworn testimony to the Jury. The statutes also contained an important section on committal whereby all witnesses whose statements were included in the dossier were required to be present when the prisoner was formally arraigned in court. Failure to continue a prosecution through non-appearance would lead to forfeit of the bond that was posted by all parties to the case, including the original plaintiff. Through this mechanism the law obligated a plaintiff to follow a case through to its conclusion, while it substituted the state for the plaintiff as soon as the initial complaint was lodged.

The committal section of the Marian statute constituted an extraordinary break with the traditions of courtroom procedure established during the Middle Ages. One of the cornerstones of a private system of criminal law had been the freedom of the plaintiff to terminate a legal action just as quickly as it had been initiated. This system obviously functioned best when the plaintiff and defendant were on familiar terms, and this was certainly a crucial component of feudal criminal law. But the committal section of the Marian code was based upon a very different set of assumptions regarding the social context in which criminal acts occurred. For it presupposed that questions of familiarity or personal vengeance could no longer dominate the scope of the judicial process. The Marian statute depersonalised the criminal justice system by removing the possibility that it could be manipulated for personal ends. And the adoption of the code no doubt reflected the fact that fewer plaintiffs now came to the authorities to lodge complaints against persons with whom they shared personal bonds.

The compilation of a written dossier also had an important effect upon the nature of courtroom procedure in criminal cases. Once the JP appeared in court with his written record he began to retreat in his role as magistrate, and instead utilised his dossier to elicit testimony in a much less arbitrary manner than previously. In essence the JP began to function as a modern prosecutor, presenting the evidence before the jury in an impartial and objective manner. This was a dramatic change from the earlier system for now a structural division had occurred between the prosecution and judging of offenders. Under the medieval system both tasks were the responsibility of the magistrate, whereas the latter task now became the province of the jury, aided by the court-room activities of the Justice of the Peace.

On the continent the prosecutorial procedures codified in the German law of 1532 and the French statute of 1539 were superficially similar to the Marian statutes, but brought about a much different courtroom procedure. The continental systems were based upon Roman-canon *Inquisitionsprozess*, an amalgam of Roman and clerical procedure that had been refined over the course of the Middle Ages as the Church became more closely involved in the prosecution of various forms of heresy. In *Inquisitionsprozess*, emphasis was also placed upon the compilation of a written dossier that would contain all the facts and observations pertinent to a particular case; this file would then serve as the evidence of record, rather than as a guide for eliciting oral testimony in court. As a result, while the Marian statutes tended over time to increase the importance of the jury within the criminal system, the continental laws minimised the participation of peers in the criminal justice process. At the same time continental procedure brought about an increase in the power of the examining magistrate. Yet, despite this difference, continental statutes also marked an important step in the shift from private to public law.

The basic advance of the sixteenth-century French and German codes rested in the disappearance of accusatory procedure and the implementation of inquisitorial procedure in the criminal justice system. This type of prosecutorial behaviour differed fundamentally from the English procedure in the following manner. While the latter system depended upon the plaintiff to maintain some interest in the affair, either freely or through coercion, the former system turned the original complaint immediately into a public issue. In France, the Ordinance of Villers-Cotterets went even further in diminishing the role of the plaintiff in criminal proceedings, making the prosecutor the sole judge of whether any particular offence merited legal intervention. In fact, under the French code, plaintiffs were allowed to be parties to a criminal case only by filing a joint civil suit. The law therefore separated the public and private aspects of criminal behaviour, making the former a state measure punishable on criminal charges, while leaving the latter as a civil matter to be adjudicated entirely outside the bounds of the criminal justice system. This was entirely different from the English system in which the plaintiff was not only an integral part of the criminal proceedings but legally bound to the case by threat of bail forfeit should he decide to withdraw his complaint.

Over the course of the sixteenth century, criminal justice systems emerged with new procedural devices that marked a clear break with the medieval traditions of criminal law. In nearly every country of Europe important changes in the criminal justice process transformed the accusatorial system of the feudal era into either the jury system adopted in England, or the inquisitorial system characteristic of the continent. In both systems the state began to replace the individual as the guiding force behind prosecutions, and this resulted in attempts to define the use and meaning of evidence, as well as a change in the general structure of courtroom and judicial procedure. All of these developments, however, could only have occurred within the context of the transformation in the philosophy of criminal law and its uses. By the sixteenth century, criminal law had completely emerged from its personalised, medieval format. Its functioning no longer rested upon familiarity and its aim was no longer to adjudicate private disputes between particular individuals. With the appearance of the state as the sole source of prosecutorial energy, the criminal act could no longer be viewed as an attack by one person on another; it was now an offence committed against society at large.

As criminal law became an aspect of state authority, one immediate result was a dramatic increase in the number of statutes, a revision of criminal definitions, and a general increase in the severity of punishments. This last development was in many respects the most significant change in criminal procedure during the early modern period for, as we have seen, the personalised nature of medieval criminal law was exemplified most clearly in the lack of harsh punishments. The relative mildness of feudal punishment followed from the fact that the system had been designed to settle disputes between equals, rather than simply to punish the guilty party. But as criminal law moved into the public domain, punishment would take on a different meaning. The primary purpose of criminal law would be to punish the criminal, while restitution to the plaintiff would ultimately become obsolete.

The new emphasis upon punishment *per se* resulted in the regular appearance of all sorts of corporal punishments in European criminal codes. Within a brief period corporal punishments became the common form of penalty, whereas they had been exceptional penalties under the feudal system. At the same time banishment and fines became less important aspects of the new statutes. Flogging, mutilation, and even execution were commonly prescribed for felonies; indeed, in some criminal codes, not a single felony was exempted from some form of corporal punishment. Public executions became frequent events and the number of persons sentenced to the gallows was now sometimes half of all those convicted of serious crimes. Various now forms of corporal punishment were introduced and in particular, torture became commonplace in most judicial proceedings.

Along with the emergence of state criminal law, the impetus toward harsher punishments was provided by the clear class character and constant increases in crime. Some means had to be found to curb the rising tide of violence and criminality that was seemingly threatening to engulf society. But, more important, something had to be done to prevent the increasing amount of crime that found the rich being victimised by the poor. Severe physical punishments were one method of inculcating discipline into the lower classes and restoring the sense of deference that had characterised feudal relations. If the poor were going to wage war on the rich through the medium of crime, then the rich could mount a defence of their interests through the medium of punishment.

Inevitably, as crime took on a class character, so did punishment. Monetary fines were still employed for various offences, but these penalties were increasingly reserved for the rich, who could still afford to settle their disputes in the traditional, personal manner. But in other respects the criminal justice system reflected the growing antipathy between the social classes that comprised European society. In England the jury ultimately excluded poor persons and individuals without vested property rights in the community. At the same time there was a general increase in the proportion of poor persons who were involved in the justice system as defendants. In France the increase in the power of the magistrate occurred at the same time that the judiciary was becoming entirely dominated by nobles of the robe and nobles of the sword. In both systems the gap between the social station of those who judged and those who were judged steadily widened. As a result both criminal law and the criminal justice system became firmly structured along class lines. Criminal procedure was not only a means for maintaining law and order, but had been transformed into a system for the maintenance of the law of one class versus the disorder of the other. In effect the criminal system was becoming a means of class control. This development reached its ultimate form in the proliferation of poor-law legislation throughout Europe.

Within a space of several decades, comprehensive schemes for dealing with the poor population were developed in every European country. In Paris the definitive Poor Law was first promulgated in 1544, having been preceded by a similar statute in Lyon in 1534. The first important legislation on paupers in England dated from 1531, while in Italy poor laws had been enacted even earlier, such as those in Venice in 1529. There were a number of reasons for this spate of ameliorative legislation. The motivation was partly religious, reflecting the social policies of certain Catholic and Protestant sects. The poor laws also had a political logic, reflecting the emergence of mercantilist doctrines alongside the appearance of the national state. Furthermore the legislation had a social basis since it was partly motivated by the generalised panic of the upper classes when confronted by so much obvious poverty in their midst. The poor laws were also a fundamental recognition of the inadequacy of clerical charity as it had been dispensed in the traditional manner. In this respect the poor laws represented a positive attempt to deal with social problems. At the same time they embodied the recognition that poverty was so widespread that its costs, even if borne by secular authorities, were simply too great to bear.

For all these reasons the new approach to poverty differed most directly from the medieval tradition in the manner in which pauperism would be defined. The Church had always assumed a position of indiscriminate alms-giving to the 'deserving poor' and justified the existence of begging in terms of the importance of charitable 'good works'. However the enormous increase in the number of paupers made distinctions about various types of poverty inconsequential when compared with the problem of simply coping with it. Now there were just too many poor persons, and the cyclical nature of work resulted in ever fresh waves of unemployed and impoverished individuals that had to be supported in some manner or other. The ancient beggar's guilds still existed, complete with their magic incantations, rituals, rigmaroles and other diversionary activities that amused people on market days. But these individuals, relatively few in number, were now joined by swarms of able-bodied folk who simply could not survive on the marginal wages available in most urban centres. The Poor Law enacted in Lyon, for example, was the direct result of the experiences of the population during the terrible spring famine of 1531. At that time thousands of persons staggered through the streets looking, in the words of a contemporary, like corpses that had escaped from the anatomical laboratory of the medical college.

Given all these factors the fundamental purpose of European poor legislation was to prevent the convergence of too many paupers within the confines of any particular town. It was quickly realised that many of the poor were recent arrivals from the countryside and would never return to their native region unless under threat of arrest. Consequently some coercive measures to prevent free movement of the poor population became the obvious solution to the problem. To attain that end, early modern poor laws abolished the distinction between deserving and undeserving poor and dealt with the manner only in terms of movement and locale. Mendicity became equated with vagabondage and the latter activity, which had always been illegal, now became a very serious crime. The criminal justice system could now be employed to deal with this new type of crime and the problem of poverty would be controlled as well. It was not by accident that a major factor in the increase in authority of the English JPs was their requirement to administer the Poor Law in the 1530s.

The appearance of poor laws had a profound effect upon the entire scope of European criminal law and punishment systems. For the poor law was, in essence, a major piece of class legislation and its essential thrust was to develop an effective method of dealing with the lower classes through some comprehensive means of social control. The poor laws of Europe could not ameliorate poverty, but they could be used as an effective method of social control, particularly when they were incorporated into the general system of criminal law. This was a fundamental point of departure in the history of criminal law and procedure because it meant that the last vestiges of private, feudal law could now be swept away. Henceforth crime and the criminal would be defined on a class basis, and in terms of the conflict between classes. Criminal law had thus become a public device in every respect, especially because it now could be used as an instrument of social policy. The rationale for criminal law was the control of crime, but crime would be defined in class terms and criminal law would be used to control that class. European criminality was about to enter its modern age.

CHAPTER 5
CRIME MOVES TOWARD ITS MODERN FORM

BEGINNING in the eighteenth century, we find that crime began to split into two distinct patterns. There was still a great deal of the older, more traditional criminality associated with the social and economic structures of the feudal world. These patterns of criminal activity, discussed in Chapter III, survived in strongest fashion in areas that lagged behind the general pace of European development. But this period also witnessed the emergence of new forms of criminality that reflected the ongoing transition to industrial life. These newer types of crime occurred most frequently in areas and among populations that were directly confronted with the effects of modernisation – places where industry and commerce developed in the earliest and most obvious sense. Sometimes both the old and new types of crime existed simultaneously within the same population, an indication that crime was a socially-indigenous activity with its own rhythms of development. However, notwithstanding the contrasts between various forms of criminal behaviour, there was a basic continuity regarding the existence of fundamental social and economic factors that provoked crime. The shape of these factors changed over time but their causal importance in the history of criminality remained intact.

The 'first cause' of crime in both the early and later period was population growth. In the earlier period we

saw that population movements – numerical and geographical – were crucial elements in the shaping of early
modern European crime. If anything this factor would
become even more important as the period wore on. For
not only did population levels change even more dramatically than ever before but the geographical mobility of
the European population would continually increase in
numbers and scope. Many people travelled further on a
regular basis than ever before and newer, larger towns
were rapidly filled with many more immigrants from the
countryside.

The social problems that began to arise as a result of
sustained population growth were signalled in contemporary opinion, perhaps the most famous being the writings of Thomas Malthus. The first edition of Malthus'
An Essay on the Principle of Population appeared in
1798 and set the tone for a prolonged debate that would
continue into the following century. However harsh and
unyielding Malthus may appear to modern readers it is
well to recall that he wrote from the vantage-point of
the results of a near-century of continuous population
growth. The result of that development had been both
the appearance of many more persons and an enormous
increase in the size of the poor population. To a certain
degree economic growth had alleviated some of the more
immediate problems caused by over-population. But during
the course of the eighteenth century, the positive effects
of economic development were diminished by inexorable
population pressure. During the first half of the eighteenth century population rose slowly in England and on
the continent, resulting in a stabilisation of the condition
of the lower classes. However from 1750 to the end of the
century this situation began to change. Although the
situation in England was less extreme, in Europe the

living standards of the lower classes declined during this period and the poor appeared, both absolutely and relatively, more numerous than ever before.

The growth of population and the generalised impoverishment of much of the lower classes had important effects upon the mode of life in both the urban and rural sectors. As to the latter, the eighteenth century saw the definitive obliteration of the remnants of rural communalism and the appearance in its place of larger commercial farms. This development was closely tied to certain economic changes but was also a primary result of the growth of the rural population. The essence of the feudal commune had been contained within a context set by limited population and a lack of mobility, thus allowing the local community to develop along self-sufficient, semi-autonomous lines. However such features could hardly survive when population greatly outpaced land supply and investment from the urban sector began to transform the structure of agriculture. Moreover the growth of population went far beyond the ability of urban centres to absorb the excess, with the result that general and widespread poverty became a feature of the rural landscape. On the eve of the Revolution of 1789, many areas in France were menaced by large bands of unemployed vagrants, most of whom were transient paupers who travelled from place to place in search of the next day's fare.

For many people the situation was becoming even more desperate in the cities. As in the countryside the population had grown at an astonishing pace and brought with it the appearance of a great many poor persons. By the end of the eighteenth century, moreover, poverty in the urban context was beginning to emerge in a much different fashion than before. During the earlier period poverty was a cyclical problem, decreasing to tolerable limits in periods of economic growth and increasing during periods of economic depression. To be sure, early modern cities always held a goodly number of paupers, but the overall levels tended to be related directly to short-term economic conditions. However this situation began to change during the later period. The size of the poor population still tended to increase in urban centres during monetary crises, such as that in England in 1766 or in Paris from 1791. At the same time a human bedrock of poverty was emerging in larger cities, spreading in mass fashion over wide areas and proving impervious either to the demands of the labour market or the threats of criminal sanctions. At the core of this group were many persons for whom traditional modes of labour held no incentive and no lure. They constituted the base of a true *lumpenproletariat* class, and it was within this group that newer forms of crime would begin to emerge.

The more traditional poor population continued to resort to crime as a means of stretching their thin allowances over the course of slack periods. As we have seen, such criminal activity, its type and extent, had long been a normal aspect of the lives of the lower classes. But crime began to serve a very different purpose for members of the *lumpen* population, most of whom viewed this activity as their only means of survival. Consequently the types and trends of these newer forms of crime were quite different from the profile of crime associated with poor populations in the past. In earlier times poverty itself had been judged a criminal offence but now the crime committed by the *lumpen* poor would be viewed as something quite apart from the pathos of their social condition.

The second basic factor that had always influenced the

course of European criminality was economic development. In Europe the overwhelming phenomenon of the eighteenth century was the slow emergence of industrial production, preceded by the commercialisation of agriculture and accompanied by an enormous increase in regional, national and international trade. The gradual transformation from workshop to factory production meant that the earlier social division of the working population would ultimately be upset. In place of the tripartite division between mercantile, commercial and service populations there slowly arose a dual division between the bourgeoisie and the labouring classes. The former was composed of the older mercantile and commercial populations while the more marginal merchants and artisans were gradually drawn into the ranks of the labouring classes. This latter development is seen quite clearly in the early history of working-class political movements, where the consciousness of factory workers was often influenced by sentiments that had their origins within the artisan population. The urban community contained many persons who did not fit into these neat categories. In many areas the old-line aristocracy survived relatively intact into the nineteenth century, exemplified by the continued existence of the German *Junkers* or the *Hidalgos* in Spain. Also, as already indicated, a vast *untervelt* maintained itself beneath the lowest ranks of the working population, indeed feeding off the working classes. But, in general terms, the urban population began to show the characteristics of a new social division, a change which occurred alongside the disappearance of many of the service-type occupations and activities that had once bound together the various sectors of the pre-industrial economy.

The reorientation of urban social structures as a result

of economic developments had its counterpart in the rural sector. Over the course of the eighteenth century, subsistence farming was replaced by commercial agricultural systems in many areas of Europe. In general, production for regional or national markets meant the enclosing of small farms, the increased specialisation of agricultural production and the gradual growth of primary industries in the countryside. These developments resulted in a dramatic change in the social composition of the rural population. Over time, rural society split into two groups: landowners (peasant or non-peasant) on the one hand, non-landowning labourers on the other. In France the percentage of non-landowning peasants had been growing steadily since the seventeenth century and, before the Revolution, the proportion of landless peasants in some zones ran as high as seventy per cent. As in the case of cities, the rural sector saw the gradual disappearance of the 'middle' class of petty proprietors, small herders and peasant craftsmen. The more enterprising members of this group were able to secure themselves in the lower ranks of the yeomen farmers, many of whom were becoming managers of large rural enterprises. The great majority of petty farmers and rural tradesmen were drawn downward, eventually to find their conditions indistinguishable from the great mass of peasants employed as day-labourers on the larger farms.

These developments did not occur with equal force throughout Europe and even by 1850 there were many rural regions that had not yet felt the effects of any commercial development. But there was no doubt that the economic and social structures of the Old Regime were beginning to pass away. In England less than 50 per cent of the active population was engaged in agriculture by 1750, and a century later the proportion of agricultural labour dropped to about one-quarter of the workforce. These developments occurred more slowly on the continent, given the slower rate of economic advance. Yet even in areas where the bulk of the population was rural-based, often a majority of the actual workforce had passed out of the agricultural sector and into proto-industrial activities.

Economic development not only brought about a shift in the occupational structure of the population but also imposed new patterns of work upon the active population. Once labour became tied to the industrial process, factory work created a different series of labouring rhythms. Now the hours of work were regular, and while work stoppages were still frequent, they were less a part of the actual labouring cycle. Work and idleness became mutually distinct, as did the factory and the home. This brought about an enormous change in family and social relations, and affected every activity, including crime. In the countryside, the commercialisation of agriculture obliterated the commune and promoted the development of migratory, as opposed to seasonal, labour. These developments also affected the entire scope of social relations and activities.

This brings us to a third and entirely new factor influencing European criminality at the end of the early modern period. Beginning in the seventeenth century and increasing in importance thereafter, politics began to play a crucial role in shaping the pattern of crime. The chief political cause of crime was the near-constant warfare in Europe that resulted in the creation and deployment of standing armies by nearly every European state. The effect of military mobilisation on crime levels took a variety of forms. First there were the excessive costs of warfare imposed upon the national population. In their most direct form these costs appeared as taxes, usually levied on essential commodities and affecting the poorest segment of the population. Indirect charges included the diversion of products away from the home market toward the troops in the field, and the inevitable inflationary spiral that occurred whenever governments engaged in costly wars. One should also not discount the effects of government economic policies during wartime. Blockades and other economic embargoes, such as the one placed on France after the Revolution, deprived the lower classes of necessary commodities and created disruptions in trade and production that brought about higher levels of unemployment. All of these factors combined to produce a serious deterioration in the living standards of the masses, and resulted in higher levels of crime.

An even more immediate political cause of crime was the effect of demobilisation when a particular conflict came to an end. Invariably the cessation of hostilities abroad increased social tensions at home, due to the return of military veterans eager to regain their place in civilian society. However, given the recessions that inevitably accompanied the end of a war, demobilised troops usually did nothing more than swell the ranks of the unemployed. In England, during the seventeenth and eighteenth centuries, there was an exact chronological coincidence between periods immediately following wars and periods of elevated crime. Criminality has been analysed in the county of Surrey from 1660 to 1800, and the peak periods, such as 1674–6, 1698–1700, 1747–51 and 1782–4, all came directly after the termination of war.[1] Contemporary opinion, including writers like Defoe and Patrick Colquhoun, were similarly convinced that periods following war saw increased crime at home.

Taking an overview of the basic factors that provoked crime, it is clear that the social environment of criminality in Europe had changed considerably from the beginning of the early modern period. Where once there had existed tiny, isolated rural settlements and an occasional small town, there now was an urbanised and relatively crowded society that was changing daily. The pace of life quickened continually and, as it did, social and economic relations became even more complicated and diverse. This is not to say that society in the earlier period was free of social problems and tensions. Rather, as the period wore on, certain types of conflicts were replaced by others and certain new social, economic and political developments would have their impact upon everyday life. We have already studied these developments from the perspective of criminality at the beginning of the early modern period. Let us now look at the later history of crime in more precise terms.

Criminal patterns in the eighteenth century exhibited some traditional characteristics together with some newer features. One basic continuity was the preponderance of various forms of theft. Perhaps the most traditional form of theft was banditry, which was still found in many outlying regions of western Europe. Although modern banditry appeared similar to its antecedents, a closer look reveals some important changes in its dynamics. In France, banditry was still common in the latter part of the eighteenth century and occurred most frequently in two quite distinct regions: the *pays de grande culture* (including parts of the Ile de France and Champagne) and the very poor region known as the Forez that lay north of Lyon. In Spain, eighteenth-century banditry was also a recurring phenomenon in two very separate zones, each one similar to a bandit region in France. Spanish bandit gangs operated on the roads that cut through La Mancha, an area not unlike the Ile de France and characterised by large, isolated farms surrounding isolated villages. Banditry was also common in the Sierra Morena, a mountainous region in Andalusia even more underdeveloped than the Forez region in France.

Banditry was endemic to all these regions because of the constant traffic between interior cities or between the interior and the coast. The impetus behind bandit activity, however, was quite different in each zone and related to the specific economic conditions faced by the local population. In the Sierra Morena and the Forez, banditry was as always indicative of backwardness, a timid and inconsequential attempt at revenge by the poor against the rich who journeyed through their midst. However, banditry in the farming regions of Champagne or La Mancha represented a wholly new development. For here bandit gangs were comprised of seasonal daylabourers who found themselves short directly following the harvest period. Sometimes banditry could provide the supplemental wage for rural labourers moving from one harvest area to another. The appearance of banditry in these regions was another indication of the gradual shift from subsistence farming toward commercial agriculture, and reflected in part a growing reliance upon a transient, seasonal labour force.

The harvest season was still an important factor in the seasonal distribution of theft in cities during the eighteenth century. In Paris, larceny always increased during the month of August, a trend for which the following explanation has been advanced. The harvest drew many wealthy landowners and their servants away from their urban dwellings and out into the countryside to supervise activities on their estates. As a result many homes containing objects of great value were often left vacant for extended periods. The demand for labour in the rural sector also drew many members of the lower classes out of the city in search of work. But for those who could not work in the countryside, there was little gainful employment to be found until the wealthier elements, as well as their workforce, returned to the city. Consequently those who remained behind during the late summer months might have turned to casual theft as a means of subsisting until the summer ended and the urban economy began to regenerate.

The extreme frequency of burglary in uninhabited domiciles was a characteristic common both to urban and to rural criminality. Even in the smallest rural settlements thieves could usually work unnoticed in the homes of the wealthier peasants, so long as they chose the correct hour and day to commit their deeds. A favourite time for illegal entry was Sunday morning, when nearly all the members of the village élite felt it incumbent upon their social station to attend mass. Another brief period that provided opportunity for larcenies of all sorts was during village festivals, occasions usually held for the purpose of demonstrating the importance and stature of the local village leaders. Such events invariably occurred out of doors, where the local notables received the homage of the rest of the community at the parish gate or in the village square. Sometimes a religious festival culminated with the entire village population marching behind an effigy to a small hermitage or other shrine located beyond the confines of the settlement. As a result homes and possessions were left unguarded and vulnerable to easy entrance and theft.

There were several reasons why rural thieves could now concentrate their activities upon wealthier members of the community. First there was a greater abundance of items of value in each community, reflecting the emergence of a rich peasant class during the shift toward commercial agriculture. Second, and perhaps more important, it was much easier than previously to dispose of luxury goods. Trade and commercial links now existed between nearly every rural hamlet and regional or national market, and journeys of even the poorest peasants to other settlements, or to nearby towns, were hardly suspect. Furthermore local communities were now constantly visited by all sorts of travelling salesmen, tradesmen, *colporteurs* (the 'fences' par excellence) and other transient peddlars, all individuals who could be enlisted to move stolen goods out of the village in foolproof fashion. The articles most frequently stolen in the countryside still indicated immediate use by the thief or his family: food, grain, cloth and other essential commodities. However, various luxury goods, including money, were also now commonly reported as missing in the aftermath of rural larceny.

The other favourite haunt of rural thieves was local trade fairs, held regularly in every region of Europe. Three aspects of fair day made it the perfect spot and time for a thief to engage in his trade. Many goods were available and displayed in such a manner that they invited theft; the population attending the fair was entirely transient and outsiders hardly noticed; the noise and general confusion disguised any variety of illegal activities. Since many fairs were organised on the basis of barter and exchange of goods rather than cash or credit sales, the handling and inspection of merchandise was not only encouraged but even recommended. It was hardly difficult for an experienced thief to examine many items and occasionally slip one into a sack or the hands of a confederate. The continuous din and bustle surrounding all activities made such behaviour difficult to detect and impossible to prevent.

The most widespread and lucrative type of rural theft, however was smuggling. This activity reached such proportions in the eighteenth century that it often embraced the collective energies of whole villages or sometimes entire counties. It is impossible to obtain any accurate figures on the number of individuals engaged in various types of smuggling, but some evidence has emerged suggesting an enormous extent of complicity in the commission of this crime. In 1745 English authorities estimated that more than 20,000 persons were continually engaged in smuggling tea along the Sussex coast, a figure not including the many more persons who received the illicit goods and passed them along. In France, tobacco smuggling involved whole rural populations to the point that police agents of the state tobacco exchange were powerless to intervene in their activities.

The popularity of smuggling was due first to the obvious profits that accrued, especially when compared to other methods of gaining a livelihood. In the areas of highest salt tax in France (*grand gabelle*), the price of salt was officially pegged at 62 *livres* per *quintal*, whereas it sold for only 5 *livres* in tax-free zones. The enormous profits that could be obtained by carrying salt from a low-tax to a high-tax region went far beyond the profits from any other form of labour. It has been estimated that one individual could make as much money in a single trip from Brittany to the Maine as he would receive for an entire month's common labour. Returns from the illicit trade in tobacco in France were almost as high because illegal tobacco could be purchased for less than half the official price.

The profits that could be derived from smuggling drew persons into this activity from all ranks of society. The smuggling of tea involved merchants as well as government officials, and was so highly organised that the costs of purchasing tea across the Channel were sometimes covered by utilising smugglers to ship wool back to the continent. This involved another whole series of illegal actions since British law prohibited the shipment of wool out of the country during the eighteenth century. In France, investment in the illicit tobacco trade came from middle-class elements and merchants, as well as from religious orders, monasteries, and even individual clerics acting on behalf of their local parishes. Often the yearly amounts of goods smuggled across national borders exceeded the volume of those products imported through legal channels.

Yet despite the entrepreneurial interest in some aspects of smuggling it remained an overwhelmingly lower-class criminal activity. This reflected a number of important developments that had occurred in parts of rural Europe during the Old Regime. First, it was indicative of the deterioration of living standards among the masses, in particular the destruction of the artisan and petty farmer class. These people had been rendered economically and socially obsolete by the economic changes of the eighteenth century, but still possessed acumen and a sense of leadership to undertake the difficult and sophisticated task of smuggling. A study of smuggling along the Sussex coast has uncovered a number of cases of smugglers who had previously been involved in related but entirely honest activities. One smuggling band leader had been a carpenter until a serious case of palsy rendered him useless in his old trade. Another large group of smugglers came from the remnants of the working population that had previously laboured in the Sussex iron furnaces. By the 1720s this industry had almost entirely disappeared, and a part of its former workforce had no doubt been drawn into the smuggling trade.

The enormous degree of lower-class involvement in smuggling also demonstrated the extent to which trade and commerce had penetrated all levels of society, allowing even the poor and labouring classes to engage in activities demanding fairly specialised commercial techniques. The tremendous popularity of smuggling was also a measure of the extreme and widespread deprivation of the lower classes that translated itself into a certain degree of class cohesion. Indeed many rural communities considered smuggling an integral and necessary part of the local economy, if only because the profits could provide the margin between survival and starvation when harvest levels fell below minimum levels. Smuggling was also a reflection of the new political realities in eighteenth-century Europe. It was a reaction to increased government levies in the form of taxes upon essential goods. In this case, social and political conditions had coincided to produce criminality on a mass scale.

Urban forms of larceny never engaged so many people or turned on such great volume, but they did exhibit certain patterns of organisation indicative of a new age. Criminal statistics from eighteenth-century Paris show that theft constituted about 85 per cent of all indicted crime from 1750 until the eve of the Revolution. The victims of larceny ran the social gamut from clerics and aristocrats to servants and other common folk. However, more than one-third of all thefts involved the taking of goods from retail shops, an activity often accomplished by means of a sales-clerk or servant passing the items over the counter to an accomplice in the street. In contrast to the countryside, where theft of immediately-disposable commodities still predominated, city theft of foodstuffs was largely confined to the open-air food markets that were established in every neighbourhood, as well as in the large wholesale depôts on the outskirts of town. But illicit entrance into personal or commercial premises was almost inevitably carried out for the purpose of securing goods of greater value: clothing, linens, silver, jewellery, and any other moveable luxury item.

In order for the urban thief to realise the value of his stolen goods, it was necessary to 'fence' or trade them for other commodities. The increase in theft in conjunction with the increased value of stolen goods gave rise to an entire secondary criminal sector revolving around the receiving and selling of purloined articles. In this milieu an important role was played by the *revendeuse*, the second-hand clothes merchant, whose domicile served as a private clearing-house for all sorts of articles of questionable origin. The old-clothes seller, often a housewife who could stay at home to meet customers, acted as a broker bringing together buyer and seller in a regular, organised fashion. The market price of any particular item was established not so much in relation to its actual value but in terms of the difficulty of disposition. The chief object of any exchange was to 'soil' the goods as soon as possible by moving them through a number of hands in order to hamper tracing and later identification. The fruits of urban larceny also could be found in the stalls at flea-markets, another form of semi-illicit enterprise that existed alongside legal markets in an organised and semi-regulated manner.

Despite the fact that two-thirds of all persons con-

victed of theft in Paris during the eighteenth century
were recent immigrants from the countryside, many of
them had developed important lines of social organisation as a means of further enhancing the possibilities of
illegal gain. Urban theft was frequently a solitary occupation, particularly as regards street crime, but in many
instances it involved the active complicity of a long chain
of individuals, running from the parlour-maid to her
delivery-boyfriend, to his streetcorner lookout, to the local
'fence', to his transient salesman partner. In this sense
the urban masses demonstrated again their ability to
organise themselves around a common task in pursuit of
a common goal.

Criminal organisation in urban centres also revolved
around the activities of gangs, who 'controlled' crime by
supervising the theft and disposal of various types of
merchandise. Perhaps the most notorious gang was that
led by Jonathan Wild, who operated in London from
1708 until his execution in 1725. Wild was the manager
of a large gang of thieves, pickpockets, house-breakers and
highwaymen, planning many of their capers, and sharing
in the return from the loot. Known as the 'Thief-Catcher
General of Great Britain and Ireland' for his willingness
to denounce rival gangs to the authorities, Wild operated
in a public manner, and even moved in 1718 to lavish
headquarters near the Old Bailey. Wild was best known
for his ability to recover stolen goods, collecting a 'fee' for
his services in return for prohibiting any local inquiry
into the circumstances of the theft. Stolen goods that
could not be returned in such a manner to their rightful
owners were often clandestinely shipped abroad or altered
and resold at home.

By the time of his execution, Wild's career had been
celebrated in verse and song. His life was the subject of

at least a dozen biographies, including those written by Defoe and Fielding. There was even a political side to his exploits. Wild's activities were compared to those of Walpole, and anti-Walpole propagandists made frequent reference to the parallel fortunes of the Great Crook and the Great Statesman. Yet his career had much more serious social implications. Even though the organisation and activities of the Wild gang were in some respects unique, they were not altogether unusual. Crime was rapidly becoming a business, a form of entrepreneurship, based upon the existence of large amounts of capital (stolen goods) and a new market (the city) in which to invest. Crime had not yet become modern, but the activities of the Wild gang and other similar criminal patterns provided the transition to the modern form.

Did crime greatly increase over the course of the eighteenth century, as contemporary opinion-makers would lead us to believe? Certainly crime levels kept pace with the increase in population, and since the latter was rising at a very fast pace we can assume that the former grew rapidly as well. But there are cogent reasons to believe that crime rates during this period actually exceeded the rate of population growth and that the increased fear of criminality among the propertied classes was related to a real, not imagined threat. Cities were rapidly filling with large numbers of persons who could find no niche in either the urban or the rural economy – the inordinate increase in female prostitution remarked on by Restif de la Bretonne and other more objective observers was a potent symptom of this phenomenon. The abundance of street crime, petty crimes of violent desperation like purse-snatchings and pickpocketing, was another hint of this new turn of events. Contemporary observers insisted that such activities were not only increasing but constituted novel forms of crime. The lack of firm data makes it impossible to find a direct connection between a growth in the size of the pauper population and a general increase in crime. Yet it is hard to believe that a correlation did not exist between these two developments.

There was another factor, however, that may have contributed to an overall increase in the level of criminality. There is no doubt that over the course of the eighteenth century there were simply more articles available to be stolen than ever before. Although the lower classes may have suffered increased poverty, this occurred in the face of an accumulation of wealth and possessions by the wealthier elements. Already great fortunes were being made on the basis of overseas trade, as well as from various types of commodity production. As a result there were plenty of goods standing about to invite theft. Contemporaries mentioned the fact that dock areas in seaport towns were constantly piled to overflowing with commodities both imported and destined for shipment overseas. After all the eighteenth century marked the time when world-wide empires were first being carved out by European commercial classes, and sea commerce was the indispensable activity for the accumulation of profits from trade. Similarly inland commerce increased as the development of home markets accentuated the commercialisation of the agricultural sector and spurred the further exchange of goods. The proliferation of industrial and commercial commodities was more than matched by the acquisition, on the part of the middle and upper classes, of luxury items to furnish their dwellings and fill their wardrobes. In fact the collection of personal merchandise occurred on a scale never previously imagined. The high fashions and expensive tastes of court life were copied to a lesser degree by everyone who had any ambition toward social pretension. There was no contradiction in great wealth existing side by side with great poverty, and the link between these two sets of circumstances was provided by the pattern of crime.

CHAPTER 6
PUNISHMENT TO FIT THE CRIME

By the seventeenth century, criminal law and procedure had moved definitely from the private to the public domain. Yet this transformation did not greatly increase either the efficacy or the impartiality of the criminal justice system. On the contrary, the triumph of public over private criminal law went hand in hand with the near-total arbitrariness of judicial action and the adoption of overwhelmingly severe punishment codes. The capriciousness of justice and the harshness of punishment were symptoms of two important developments that shaped the modern criminal justice system in Europe: the structure of governmental authority, and the necessity of developing a means of controlling and disciplining the lower classes. During the seventeenth century Absolutism had emerged in its classic form. This was the period when the problem of criminal disorder on a mass scale first became acute. In Chapter IV we saw how these two factors influenced the beginnings of the early modern criminal justice system. The purpose of this chapter is to view how that system began evolving towards its modern form.

Perhaps the most instructive method for detailing the administration of public criminal law would be to recount a typical criminal case. The incident in question occurred in Milan in 1630, and served as the subject of Alessandro Manzoni's nineteenth-century essay, *The Column of*

Infamy.[1] The case concerned a young civil servant who was accused of smearing a 'foul substance' on the wall of several homes and thus endangering the health and lives of all the residents in the neighbourhood. The defendant, Guglielmo Piazza, was arrested on the basis of the testimony of two eye-witnesses. He was interrogated by the Chief of Police and, unbeknown to him, his house was searched. At the conclusion of the session with the Chief of Police, during which Piazza denied being in the vicinity of the crime four different times, he was sent back to jail and the case was forwarded to the presiding magistrate. However, having denied the accusations of his interrogator, Piazza then faced the charge of having lied to the Court, since the magistrate could not believe that an individual could deny the validity of two eye-witness accounts. Having failed to gain a confession from the defendant the authorities subjected him to lengthy torture until he finally implicated an accomplice in the scheme. The unfortunate man had still not admitted to any wrong-doing; he simply agreed with the suggestion of his torturers that he had met a certain individual at a certain point whom he believed was totally unconnected with the charges being pressed against him. The constable then arrested the second individual, a barber named Mora, submitted him to torture, and forced him under threat to reimplicate Piazza. Further torture of both men produced several more names that the Court could involve as accomplices in the criminal act. It should be noted that two persons were now under indictment for a serious crime but did not know the nature of the charges against them, nor were they aware of the arrest of each other.

The confessions of the two individuals were presented to the magistrate who decreed the following sentence:

each man to be brought to the place of execution in a cart, his body stuck with red-hot pokers as the cart moved through the streets, his hands chopped off, his torso broken on the rack, his throat cut and the corpse burnt. Thus two men, perhaps totally innocent of the crime of which they were charged, would be put to death in the most brutal fashion. The case had been constructed out of unsubstantiated eyewitness testimony, illegal entry and search, torture and false confession.

The case was described in detail by Manzoni as a vehicle for advocating the restructuring of the criminal justice system. Yet the description of the trial and execution of Piazza and Mora was entirely and accurately representative of criminal procedure and justice as it functioned under the Old Regime. The system in Milan and elsewhere was entirely arbitrary at all levels. Methods for collecting evidence included invasion of privacy, spying, unsubstantiated denunciations and secret interrogations. The chief judicial officer exercised enormous discretion in nearly every aspect of the process and could adopt procedures and impose penalties without precedent.

The worst aspect of the system was the indiscriminate use of torture against defendants, even when the individual was completely ignorant of the charges brought against him. The rationale behind torture was that it constituted a simple means of gaining a confession and eliminated costly investigatory activity for which there was no competent staff available. The question of truth versus falsity was rarely at issue. Rather the problem was to determine the guilt or innocence of the accused. Yet the system proceeded from an initial premise that the alleged wrongdoer was indeed guilty of the offence for which he was being tried. Otherwise he would not have been denounced! In effect the total burden of proof fell upon the defendant, an almost impossible task considering that no defence attorneys were ever present and that the authorities frequently failed to inform the prisoner of the alleged crime. From the point of view of the Court, therefore, torture became the most efficient means for forcing the defendant to admit his guilt, which the entire system assumed to be self-evident. This viewpoint turned the basic precept of medieval criminal procedure on its head. For under the medieval system, the guilt of the alleged defendant was rarely an important aspect of the affair. Now the question of guilt was the sole issue before the Court.

The basic reason for the exercise of this unchecked judicial power was that the Court represented the sovereign, and the criminal law had become an effective means of extending state power into local and private affairs. The magistrate was a representative of the Monarch: if the Crown was above the law then its chief law officers could not be bound to respect it either. The capricious nature of judicial authority was also a means for substituting the authority of the sovereign over local customs and traditions, since courtroom practice could not be held in check either by accepted local practices or conformity to local beliefs and traditions of justice. The arbitrary character of the criminal justice system was also related to the fact that criminal law was slowly moving into previously non-criminal domains. Just as civilian authorities had assumed the burden of dispensing charity, for example, so they also extended criminal law to cover religious conduct and other areas of private conscience.

The extensive use of torture had a rationale all its own. As described by Manzoni, torture became a commonplace feature of nearly every criminal procedure. The defendant and his accomplices were now subject to a great degree of physical brutality, and court proceedings were often suspended while a recalcitrant defendant was taken down to the torture chamber to be further coerced. Although rules governing civil torture retained the clerical admonition protecting the life of the victim from the excesses of his torturer, the methods employed in criminal cases to inflict pain were far more extreme than those utilised in ecclesiastical proceedings. This is because religious torture was often used as a form of penance, in which the victim was made to feel humiliated through submitting to a mild form of physical or mental punishment. However no such philosophy was employed to ameliorate the torture associated with the criminal justice systems of western Europe. Rather it was believed that more severe forms of torture would bring about quicker confessions and, equally important, provoke the defendant to implicate many other individuals.

The use of torture could also not be separated from an increase in the severity of criminal punishment under the Old Regime. As the criminal justice system moved away from its original form, i.e. as a means of adjudicating disputes among equals, it became more and more a class-based system. Consequently the legal and moral restraints upon the use of physical force in punishments started to disappear. At the same time the upper classes condoned and supported brutality against the masses, especially as criminal law became an effective method for imposing social control. The use of corporal punishments and torture was also viewed as a necessity in the absence of police forces; thus punishments themselves were seen as a means of controlling crime. Only in England did the grand jury system and the open trial procedure largely inhibit the use of torture in criminal proceedings. Yet

English criminal law would ultimately embody the most severe punishment code in Europe.

Finally, torture and severe punishments became part of the ideology of criminal law which sought to impart a genuine sense of respect for authority amongst the lower classes. The brutality of punishment was a function of its public nature; the populace would *feel* the weight of power and authority as they heard the dying man's screams and saw his body torn apart. It is important to remember that Old Regime philosophies of punishment did not yet recognise the punitive element in penalties, this conception coming later in the writings of Enlightenment reformers. Punishment, as in the early period, still had a symbolic function although it now symbolised a very different state of affairs.

For all these reasons it is quite clear why Voltaire would consider the Old Regime criminal code in France to have been 'planned to ruin citizens'.[2] For its arbitrary nature and gross abuse of morality threatened the welfare of all members of the community. This was seized upon by contemporary thinkers because the rights of the community, as opposed to those of the sovereign, had become the crucial philosophical and political issue of the eighteenth century. Consequently, when political and moral theorists studied society from the point of view of equal rights for all citizens, the criminal justice system came under immediate attack. It was quickly realised that the rights of the community could only be guaranteed if the unrestricted power of the sovereign could be curtailed, a power manifest most obviously in the law. Foremost among the complaints of reformers was the gross abuse of torture. This was seen by Montesquieu and others as the most blatant reflection of absolutist despotism and one requiring immediate reform. Just as the political thought of Hobbes served to defend Absolutism and support Old Regime criminal procedure, the theories of Montesquieu and Voltaire attacked Absolutism and censured its methods of administering criminal law.

In attempting to rationalise criminal procedure, however, Enlightenment criminal reformers faced one serious problem. Although any successful revision of criminal codes demanded the application of the doctrine of equality, this could not be extended to the point of abolishing class distinctions. On the contrary, a humane and efficient criminal justice system was seen as a perfect means of guaranteeing harmony in a society based unalterably upon concrete differences in status and wealth. Consequently it was not the class-bound nature of the system that offended eighteenth-century thinkers. Rather it was the various abuses of the system that occurred as feudal law was reshaped to fit the necessities of the absolute state. The doctrine of 'equality before the law' meant that justice should be administered on a rational, effective basis regardless of the extent to which law constituted the cornerstone of class privilege. This was the essential reasoning behind Montesquieu's critique of torture. Its use did not make the system more efficient, nor did it make the victim more disposed to leading a lawful existence. In fact such methods only made it more difficult to administer the law in a rational manner.

The decisive Enlightenment breakthrough in the area of criminal procedure occurred, however, in Italy with the publication in 1764 of *Dei delitti et delle pene* (*Of Crimes and Punishments*) by Cesare Bonesana, Marchese di Beccaria.[3] The author was a member of the Lombard aristocracy that oversaw the reforms of the House of Austria in northern Italy. As a result of the connection with Vienna this local elite was receptive to Enlightenment ideas, and Beccaria in fact belonged to a literary club, *l'Accademia dei Pugni*, which discussed works written by French *philosophes*. Although Beccaria was just twenty-five when he began to write *Dei delitti*, he was already steeped in the writings of Montesquieu and Voltaire. He published it anonymously, but within a year the work and its author had achieved a stunning success. *Dei delitti* was by no means the first work on criminal justice to be published in Europe. It did, however, strike out on an entirely new path. For unlike earlier works which were largely commentaries on existing laws, Beccaria's approach was much more fundamental and, at the same time, universal in scope. This method, as some scholars have suggested, was the only means of making an impact on the Italian legal community since any legal philosopher had to cope with the full weight of the Roman legal tradition. Consequently one could not deal with the issue in specific, micro-legal terms and hope to move opinion very far. The only effective approach was to write polemics and seek controversy.

Beccaria's theories regarding criminal justice can be divided into five general parts: purpose, procedure, punishment, responsibility and prevention. As to the overall purpose of criminal law, Beccaria believed that law should not be used to prohibit certain behaviour, but simply as society's method of regulating certain necessary activities. This represented a distinct break with the earlier period when criminal law reform had always involved the expansion of statutes to cover every conceivable situation. Beccaria's insistence on this point was in some measure due to the fact that as a Milanese, he was well aware of the disadvantages of lengthy, cumbersome law-codes such as the *Carolina*.

Regarding administration and specific criminal procedure, Beccaria reversed the traditional concept that had served as a cornerstone of Old Regime criminal law by insisting upon the innocence of the accused until proven guilty. This principle led him to denounce all the procedural excesses illuminated by Manzoni's little text, including secret interrogation, unsubstantiated testimony, false evidence and, most of all, torture. The statutes utilised in any criminal justice system should be clear and should contain unalterable sentences for each crime. This would establish the sovereignty of the law over the courtroom magistrate (and Monarch) and eliminate much of the arbitrariness of criminal procedure. Finally there should exist a complete and public record of all laws that could be used as a basic reference by all citizens in order to judge the effectiveness of judicial administrators.

The third basic issue discussed by Beccaria was punishment. Punishment was to be retributive, and in this respect Beccaria was well in keeping with the post-feudal tradition. However, he broke with that tradition by advocating the end of capital punishment for all crimes. The most suitable form of punishment was imprisonment, and this course was advocated for several reasons. Imprisonment was the only type of punishment that could be made to fit the crime exactly by gradations in the length of sentences. It was also a sure method for equalising punishment between those with and without the means to pay a fine, since the former would now be subject to the same penalties as the latter. Finally, imprisonment was a *certain* form of punishment and this was a crucial aspect of Beccaria's system. Punishment had not only to be prescribed in a clear manner for every offence, but it also had to be meted out on a swift and uncompromising basis. Furthermore, once sentenced, the prisoner had to undergo the punishment; there could be no possibility of appeal or reprieve. Imprisonment was thus the most rational method for attaining all those desired ends.

Concerning views of crime and criminals, Beccaria took what for modern readers might be a harsh and uncompromising position, but one that was perfectly logical within the system that he advocated. He rejected any moral considerations in judging the criminal, nor was he willing to take personal or background factors into account in determining the degree of guilt or required punishment for any particular crime. This was a significant departure from the immediate post-feudal period when the system had encouraged all sorts of judicial reprieves and pardons based upon benefit of clergy, military service, or other forms of plea-bargaining. However, as we have seen, many of these local customs of magnanimous justice had been discarded during the seventeenth century, and Beccaria's insistence upon the full, personal responsibility of the offender was a reflection of that change.

The final aspect of Beccaria's system concerned the prevention of crime. Here the author put his complete trust in a just and rational system of law and procedure not only as a means of punishing criminals but also as the most effective deterrent of crime. While the rejection of any police force might appear totally irrational to modern criminologists, this position was in keeping with eighteenth-century thought. Beccaria viewed the police with scepticism, because he could not believe that a police force would have any loyalty except to the Crown. Moreover he was afraid to grant unchecked police authority to an institution whose members had always shown themselves willing to violate the letter and the spirit of the law. And these violations had been the hallmarks of police methods under the Old Regime. The police had been the torturers and had practised all the unjust and immoral methods of surveillance and detention that Enlightenment thinkers abhorred.

For eighteenth-century philosophers, the liberal position enunciated by Beccaria provided the answer to a basic and fundamental social problem. On the one hand there was the obvious necessity to create a system that would serve as an effective deterrent to the growing criminality of the masses. On the other hand this deterrent force should not be so abused as to violate basic human rights that were only just being awarded to the bourgeoisie. It was therefore absolutely essential to preserve the criminal justice system along class lines, although the political exigencies of the period forced liberals to demand the abolition of the more gross and obvious manifestations of class justice. Beccaria provided the vital synthesis by linking a decrease in the severity of punishment with the concept of individual responsibility for criminal acts. This was the essence of the dictum 'equal justice before the law'. This thesis assumed an equality of treatment, but more important, an equality of social circumstances. The modern criminal justice system had thus invented a social fiction in order to disguise its legal fictions.

We should not, however, discount the positive effects of Beccaria's thought, even in terms of the treatment of common criminals. Beccaria's writings were an important factor in the reform of certain criminal codes, including the abolition of capital punishment in Tuscany. To a certain extent his ideas were a reflection of the actual course of events: torture was being discarded in many European countries, and the evolution of the modern law of proof rendered torture irrelevant to criminal procedure. These developments were still tentative, and were granted an intellectual foundation through the force and persuasion of Beccaria's remarks. In the long run his views on crime and punishment would mark an important step forward in the field of criminology, particularly his insistence upon a systematised method of courtroom procedure and methods of punishment. Indeed most of his observations and diagnoses of the criminal justice system remain entirely relevant today.

Like most intellectual tracts, however, the public reaction to Beccaria's work far exceeded the actual degree of implementation. In fact, at the time he was writing, criminals probably faced the most severe and brutal system of punishments in the history of European criminality. Beginning at the end of the seventeenth century, but continuing into the eighteenth, the death sentence was extended to cover all sorts of offences, even those of the most trivial sort. In France nearly every type of larceny was punishable by death, regardless of the value of the stolen goods. *Vol en grand chemin* resulted in the death of the highwayman at the site of the crime or the capture. *Vol avec effraction* (breaking and entering) was punishable with death by hanging, especially if there had been any sort of violence during the commission of the crime. For *vol simple* (simple larceny) the penalty varied according to circumstances, but a theft of goods valued at more than 10 *livres* could result in a capital sentence in certain regions of France.

It was in England, however, that the death penalty was extended to cover nearly every sort of crime, particularly any offence associated with the theft of property and real goods. In 1689 there were about 50 offences punishable by death, and this number had increased to more than 200 by the end of the eighteenth century. English law was revised to include 33 new capital crimes during the reign of George II, and another 63 capital crimes were added to the statute books during the last forty years of the century. The most crucial legal step was taken in 1723 when the Waltham Black Act was first passed in Parliament. It was extended over a series of re-enactments and its provisions became part of the permanent criminal code in 1758. The Waltham Black Act made it a capital offence to trespass or poach in the King's forests throughout the realm. Further it shortened criminal procedure and denied defendants recourse to trial by jury in many cases. The procedural and punitive provisions of the Waltham Act were successively extended to cover all sorts of criminal offences. Nearly every time that Parliament enacted a law regulating trade or commerce, for example, it appended a rider calling for capital punishment in cases of crime related to that particular economic activity. By the end of the century, at least in theory, English property was protected by the most comprehensive system of capital punishment statutes ever devised.

It is still difficult to understand what lay behind the mania for capital punishment in the English parliament during the eighteenth century. A recent scholar of the Waltham Acts could not discover a single serious incident in 1723 that might have motivated the lawmakers into first legislating such dire codes. In fact the original Act was passed with a minimum of debate at a time when the Commons was rarely unanimous about anything. Furthermore the later extensions of the Waltham Act were passed with similarly little argument and the only serious and prolonged discussion about the Act's import came on its final abolition in 1823. Thus the Black Acts would appear to have no logical explanation, especially since so many contemporaries, including the eminent

Blackstone, were arguing for criminal reform. The answer lies most clearly in the general political and philosophical attitudes held by members of parliament during the eighteenth century. They were concerned primarily to protect property and the rights of the propertied classes. They believed that criminal law was one instrument through which these beliefs could be effectively expressed. And finally they knew that many of the capital statutes were disregarded in the course of actual sentencing.

As more crime became eligible for capital punishment, the number of felons actually executed either remained stationary or declined in absolute terms. This meant that relative to the constant increase in statutory provision for execution the number of executions declined throughout most of the eighteenth century. Why were so few people put to death when the obvious intention of the Commons was to extend the death penalty into nearly every area of crime? We do not have a precise answer, although the most obvious factor was the growing popularity of other forms of punishment. In the earlier period, the lower classes faced either execution or various forms of corporal punishment. Common criminals were usually too poor to pay fines and did not possess the economic or political means to secure a pardon. Yet by the eighteenth century the growth of the western economy, the need for manpower on the part of the national state and the development of overseas empires all created the need for manpower that could be met partially through the use of convict labour. Thus certain forms of punishment, like incarceration in workhouses, galley slavery and transportation to bleak, colonial areas served a much more rational end than did execution.

The modern form of banishment – transportation – became an important aspect of criminal punishment in

the eighteenth century, particularly in those countries
that were beginning to construct colonial systems abroad.
The need for cheap labour in the colonies, combined with
overpopulation at home, resulted in the frequent use of
transportation in eighteenth-century punishment systems.
In Paris before the Revolution, twice as many convicts
were transported as were sentenced to galleys, and the
ratio rose to 7 to 1 as regards those sentenced to death.
In England the number of transported also ran well ahead
of the number sentenced to capital punishment, and
many of the latter had their sentences commuted to
transportation as well.[4] Even countries that did not
possess overseas empires often sold their convicts to other
countries in order to transport them abroad. In the
eighteenth century German authorities sent some of their
prisoners to North America as slaves, while somewhat
later, Prussia sent convicted felons to Russia to labour in
Siberia.

Although capital punishment was utilised much less
frequently in practice than in statute, an occasional
execution nonetheless served a variety of important purposes. At a time when society's leaders considered the
masses unruly and in need of discipline, a public execution
became a potent reminder of the authority of the State,
manifested in its ability to exact the ultimate penalty
from any one of its citizens. Indeed when the event was
dressed up in all its pomp and ceremony it became a
spectacular occurrence. As Dickens described the scene
prior to Fagin's execution: 'Everything told of life and
animation but one dark cluster of objects in the centre of
all – the black stage, the cross-beam, the rope, and all the
hideous apparatus of death'.[5] The horror was magnified at
the end of the eighteenth century, because the unruliness
of the mobs at the scaffold necessitated the stationing of

large numbers of troops at the scene. The presence of the army in full battle dress lent an even more sombre tone to the proceedings.

In the end Beccaria's dictum regarding swift and equal justice could only be observed by finding some other means of punishing the great majority of criminals. Moreover transportation was simply becoming too great a burden for colonial economies to bear. At the beginning colonial areas had been bereft of manpower, since supplies were scarce and investment was minimal in anything except trade. Consequently convict labour could be used to open up new colonial areas for later and more intensive development. However, once a colonial economy developed to the point of attracting free labour from the mother country and other places, convict labour was no longer a productive enterprise. By the nineteenth century most colonial administrators demanded that convict transportation be largely curtailed or abolished altogether. These demands paralleled events in Europe where for other reasons, the labour of convicted felons was also being terminated. The view that convict labour was no longer productive in the traditional sense was connected with the emergence of penitentiaries and the modern punishment system. We will discuss those developments after looking at the emergence of modern crime.

CHAPTER 7
THE BEGINNINGS OF MODERN CRIME

THE social and economic factors that had influenced the course of criminality in the eighteenth century accelerated in force in the period leading up to 1850. Population growth and economic development had succeeded in bringing about a new social structure and, in particular, had resulted in a thoroughgoing urbanisation of many new zones. This transition toward a modern social structure was most pronounced in Britain, a country that had contained only two cities of more than 50,000 inhabitants in 1750, but held eight urban centres of that size by 1801. Moreover, during the next fifty years, the number of urban centres with populations of more than 50,000 rose to twenty-nine, including nine cities that now contained more than 100,000 persons. Some of these places had grown up extremely rapidly. Manchester had a population of only about 25,000 persons in the 1770s, increasing to 70,000 by 1800, but then jumping to 200,000 in 1830 and 250,000 by the middle of the century. Other regions in Europe lagged behind England's startling urban growth, but the overall pattern was similar. France had only three cities of more than 100,000 persons in 1800, but by 1850 two more cities had reached that size and many provincial centres were also becoming heavily populated. Even in Spain, a country characterised by the preponderance of rural underdevelopment, urbanisation 'took off' in the first half of the nineteenth century, with ten cities doubling their population between 1800 and 1850, while urban population increased from 10 per cent to 20 per cent of the national total.

It was not just the size of urban centres in the nineteenth century that contrasted so clearly with the earlier period. It was also the appearance of so much obvious urban poverty in the apparent face of economic development. A census of London taken in 1851, when the city contained better than one million persons, shows that just about half the population reported no certifiable trade occupation or means of employment – and this was the state of affairs in the city that ranked as the commercial and economic centre of the entire world! The area of Manchester-Salford contained more than 400,000 persons, but many of its neighbourhoods presented a dismal picture of grinding poverty. Here is how one working-class slum was described by Engels in 1844: 'Some four thousand people, mostly Irish, inhabit this slum. The cottages are very small, old and dirty, while the streets are uneven, partly unpaved, not properly drained and full of ruts. Heaps of refuse, offal and sickening filth are everywhere interspersed with pools of stagnant liquid. The atmosphere is polluted by the stench and is darkened by the thick smoke of a dozen factory chimneys. A horde of ragged women and children swarm about the streets and they are just as dirty as the pigs which wallow happily on the heaps of garbage and in the pools of filth.'[1]

Allowing for a degree of exaggeration on the part of the observer (he was speaking about the Irish, after all), this description was by no means unique to Manchester. There was no lack of similar examples from the continent. The city of Naples contained more than half a million people, and its slums stretched from the wharves and into every area of the town. The southern part of Madrid likewise contained an enormous population of human rejects, whose pitiful existence would be captured at the end of the nineteenth century in the writings of Baroja and Valle Inclán. These were the social conditions that had been spawned by a combination of population increase and unplanned economic development.

One of the most crucial elements in this new urbanisation was the gradual division that occurred between those persons we call the working poor, as distinct from those whom the system had rendered altogether useless. This latter group, the *lumpen*, had begun to emerge in the eighteenth century, but by the following epoch they constituted a true sub-culture of poverty with their own traditions and even their own historical roots. The creation of the lumpen had been a long process, but it was accelerated by the same economic and social forces that brought Europe into the Industrial Age. Above all, the lumpen class was a product not of backwardness but of progress; it was the human waste produced by the social transformation that accompanied the emergence of industrial capitalism.

The lumpen included peasants who had been forced off their land by enclosures and rack-renting, workers discharged from small workshops that disappeared in the wake of mass enterprise, servants dismissed from the homes of indebted gentlemen, and labourers or other marginal workers from all sorts of pre-industrial business concerns. Many persons from these groups did not wind up as rejects, but became part of the growing industrial workforce that inhabited the proletarian neighbourhoods of every large city. As we have recently begun to appreciate, they survived by developing a sense of solidarity which blended their older traditions with new ideas and practices more applicable to the rigours of the modern age. But other members of these groups were unable, for personal and social reasons, to find a place in the new scheme of things. Over time these people could not be considered unemployed, because they possessed no sense of work as an alternative mode of existence. Rather they became part of the army of the streets, existing in a loose and semi-organised fashion at the base of the social pyramid.

The proletariat as it developed as a class was surrounded by human parasites, persons who fed off it in many different ways. Every working-class neighbourhood had its collection of petty-bourgeois shopkeepers and tradesmen who committed a sort of legalised crime upon their clientele by short-weighting and overcharging for inferior goods. The corner ale-house offered cheap spirits at high prices and the local Shylock offered quick loans at exorbitant rates. This was the element in working-class communities that employed the lumpen on a casual basis only to carry out a variety of odd and disreputable tasks. Many of these tasks were in reality various sorts of crimes, but perpetrated in an accepted and therefore legal manner. The Shylock needed his collector, the tavern owner needed his bouncer, and such occupations were always awarded to members of the lumpen class.

It is therefore not surprising that most of the victims of street crimes committed by members of this lumpen criminal class were also members of the lower classes. In fact many of these crimes were nothing more than extensions of the type of 'legal' activities to which the lumpen were drawn. The working poor had little to offer in the way of precious goods; similarly they could mount only a slight defence against the predations of crime. The physical environment of the working-class slum provided endless avenues of concealment and escape for the criminal; dark alleys, narrow winding stairs, rooftops and garrets presented a maze of passageways that could be used for flight from the scene of a crime. These physical features were also noticed, reconnoitred and catalogued by members of the lumpen population. This was their occupation, and they had the time to do it with great care.

The discipline imposed upon the labouring population by the factory system also made the criminal's lot less hazardous. Factory work took people out of the home on a regular basis. Whole families arose and decamped every morning in order to spend another full day in the mill. Small children were left unattended at home during the day, or herded together in a single home under the watchful eye of an elderly person. Most work was done on shifts; the workday began at the same hour each morning and night. Consequently a thief could effect, unmolested, an illegal entrance into any number of workingmen's houses if he knew the labouring patterns of the inhabitants. By the second decade of the nineteenth century, larceny accounted for more than three-quarters of all reported crime in England; while this was an exceptionally high proportion of the overall criminal pattern, continental criminality exhibited a similar profile. Of this total, less than ten per cent of the reported thefts involved the taking of merchandise from shops. Notwithstanding constant complaints about the activities of thieves in well-to-do establishments, the great bulk of all thefts involved the taking of possessions from the poor.

We must be careful not to draw the line too carefully between the working as opposed to the non-working poor. The differences in real life were never as stark or vivid as contemporary opinion or more recent social accounts would lead us to believe. Nevertheless, in the popular mentality, nineteenth-century criminality was now associated entirely with a specific criminal population, distinct in mores, dress, modes of conduct and even geographical location. It was this last element that lent a certain credibility to the view that there existed a separate criminal class. Every large town contained criminal neighbourhoods inhabited only by members of this particular population. Within many English cities these areas were known as rookeries, and often located just beyond the city limits, as in the case of St. Giles outside London. Yet sometimes the most notorious haunts were found in the middle of a town. In Manchester the most infamous rookery, Charter Street, was a narrow, alley-like lane running right through the centre of the city. One of the significant features of the environment of the rookery was the large number of children, and particularly young boys, who served as apprentices or mascots to the older criminals. Usually these children ended up in the rookeries as a result of abandonment by their parents or parental deaths. Their existence in such great numbers (provoking endless comment in the popular literature) was clear evidence of the negative effects of modernisation.

Contemporaries were convinced of the existence of a professional criminal class by the 1830s, if not earlier, and took great care to distinguish between crimes committed by professional criminals and those resulting from the criminality of the labouring class. The latter activity, it was thought, was evidently a by-product of short-term distress, an act of desperation by persons who would never indulge in such behaviour except in moments of extreme crisis. Professional crime, on the other hand, was an entirely different phenomenon, related only indirectly to the poverty of the lower classes, and considered to be a social problem in and of itself. In fact it was believed that professional criminals came from a population whose existence was a *cause* of greater impoverishment of society as a whole. Despite the extent to which contemporary observers confused the new criminality by viewing the effect as the cause, their attitudes none the less represented an awareness of the profound change that had occurred in the character of the lower-class population.

The professional criminal class was divided into many sub-groups, each with its own criminal speciality, each operating within a certain milieu, each devising a specific set of customs and habits in order to effect its illegal tasks. Over the course of the entire period a new language grew up and served as a means of identifying various forms of criminal activity, as well as a code of communication among the criminal population. In London pickpockets included 'buzzers', who stole handkerchiefs from men's pockets, 'wires', who picked women's pockets, 'prop-nailers', who stole pins and brooches, and 'thimble-screwers', who specialised in grabbing watches off chains. Many other picturesque terms were applied to cover a wide variety of criminal activities. Thieves who frequented railway stations were called 'drag sneaks' or 'snoozers', the latter referring to those individuals who slept in the station at night in order to prey upon the early morning traffic. The most imaginative set of expressions was applied to the various forms of burglary. The 'star-glazer' cut panes out of shop-windows as a means of entering commercial premises, while 'cracksmen' generally entered private homes. The criminal class even extended its slang to cover its own anatomy. In France criminals sardonically distinguished between the *sor-*

bonne and the *tronche*. In popular lingo the *sorbonne* was the head that contained a criminal brain, a unique species of cerebellum. But the *tronche* referred to the same head at the moment it was severed from the body by the guillotine and became no different from the head of any law-abiding citizen.

The *modus operandi* of the professional criminal class exemplified the spirit in which they viewed their work, for most crimes were committed with the use of accomplices, and reflected a high degree of planning and practice prior to the actual execution of the crime itself. A common device employed by store-thieves was to have several confederates create a rumpus in front of an establishment, while a third or fourth member of the group would enter the premises. As the storekeeper hurried outside to investigate the disturbance, the 'inside man' would rifle the till or take valuable goods. Another similar method consisted of no more than an alleged inability to find an item that had 'accidentally' fallen on the floor. While several persons would distract the shopkeeper into searching for the item, another party would stealthily move behind the counter and effect the theft.

Another type of crime that became increasingly prevalent during this period consisted of mugging or other violent types of theft in which the victim was unable to comprehend or stop the attack. Many thieves made their living from stealing valuables or even clothing from drunkards. These criminals, called 'bug-hunters', could be found loitering outside taverns or near cheap boarding-houses that catered for the growing number of indigent alcoholics in urban slums. The population that resided in boarding-houses was particularly susceptible to this kind of attack. Often alone in the city, without friends and possessing only scant resources, boarding-house patrons could be lured into a variety of dangerous situations, especially when caught unawares on the way home from the local saloon. As Dickens says in *Martin Chuzzlewit*: 'To tell of half the queer old taverns that had a drowsy and secret existence near Todger's [the lodging-house] would fill a goodly book.'[2]

We usually associate boarding-house life with a tarnished, lower middle-class respectability, the establishment presided over by such matronly figures as Madame Vauquer from *Old Goriot* or Mrs. Tibbs in *Sketches by Boz*. However, the reality of boarding-house life was usually quite different from these literary images. The population within such establishments was usually quite poor, the majority of such houses located in slum areas, and crimes of all sorts were regularly committed on the premises. Indeed lodging-houses were considered one of the favourite haunts of professional criminals, and every rookery had several local hotels for transients. It was also common knowledge that lodging-houses served as fronts for brothels, and these establishments were often found within or close by the most notorious rookeries in the city.

Nineteenth-century commentators invariably said that the new, professional crime embodied two characteristics which distinguished it from the older, more traditional forms of criminality. First, many crimes were committed involving deceit or trickery in order to disguise the identity and methods of the criminal as well as to obscure the criminal act. Observers constantly remarked on the fact that the criminal population of the rookeries displayed many different forms of dress in order to go out into the city and not attract attention within the milieu in which they chose to operate. Men could be observed dressed in fancy waistcoats and linen stockings, enabling them to stand inconspicuously in a well-dressed theatre crowd as they rifled pockets during the intermission crush. Others would don the working-clothes of chimney-sweeps, allowing them to operate relatively unmolested on the rooftops of private residences. Still another favourite disguise was to pose as a delivery-boy, thus facilitating the entry and reconnoitring of an exclusive, private residence.

The use of disguises by professional criminals was an important element in the contemporary analysis of criminality. The ability to devise a disguise reflected careful long-range planning of the crime, as well as an awareness of the possible hazards posed by the particular undertaking. The disguise also demonstrated that the criminal had spent time observing his victim, possibly comparing notes with like-minded observers, in order to leave little or nothing to chance. For all these reasons the commission of crimes by costumed criminals confirmed the contemporary belief in the existence of a professional, criminal class. Crimes of desperation provoked by an immediate need never exhibited such careful and precise premeditation. To the contrary, the typical criminal activity of an unemployed worker usually began with begging in the streets and escalated to petty larceny on the spur of the moment if adequate alms could not be collected by the end of the day. In fact what contemporaries called casual crime, the criminality of the working poor, could not develop from a pre-planned scheme, if only because casual criminals had been too busy working to think in such terms.

The second characteristic of professional, as opposed to amateur criminality, was the frequent employment of several confederates in order to effect the illicit act. Traditionally street crime provoked by hunger or unemployment was an individual affair, and for that reason the perpetrator was usually caught immediately. However, professional crime was frequently committed on a group basis, the gang never being large enough to draw attention to itself, but never so small that any of its members would be left isolated or unprotected. The occurrence of group crime was another new phenomenon persuading contemporaries that they were now confronted by a professional criminal class. It was impossible to believe that a crime not planned well in advance could involve decoys, lookouts and other types of accomplices in order to ensure the success of the action. It was assumed that full-time criminals spent as much time planning their escape from the scene as they spent planning the crime itself.

There were certain newer forms of criminality in which both deceit and group planning were absolutely essential to the nature of the crime. One such activity was fraud, particularly in the form of counterfeiting and forgery. These activities assumed quite large dimensions in societies where a cash economy was beginning to permeate all levels of economic exchange. Indeed, criminal statistics for England show that there were more indictments for counterfeiting and forgery annually than for mugging, housebreaking, horse theft, and the combined totals for murder, manslaughter and rape. These crimes of fraud constituted the quintessential proof that a professional criminal class had come into being, complete with an army of technicians and sophisticated equipment.

Just as there had been a gradual transformation in the structure of the mass population, so there had been a shift in the profile of crime and a change in contemporary attitudes towards the criminal. To be sure, a majority of all criminal acts were still the traditional, petty, spur-of-the-moment affairs that had always predominated in the criminal pattern of any society. But this reflected the fact that crime was always somewhat endemic to the lower-class population, regardless of the social contours of that class. Yet there still had developed a clear awareness on the part of the establishment that crime had begun to change its form, and this growing consciousness provoked several interesting analyses of the situation.

On one hand, a significant body of opinion held that crime committed by the working poor, in contrast to professional criminality, could be tolerated since the perpetrator turned to unlawful behaviour in the temporary absence of more lawful pursuits. The criminality of the labouring class was considered simply as an extension of begging, which was the only means of survival for unemployed workers. As Henry Mayhew remarked: 'There can be no doubt that in terms of hardship many honest labourers are forced into the streets to beg. A poor hardworking man, whose children cry to him for food, can feel no scruple in soliciting charity.' Yet false begging was also a common tactic of professional criminals, and it was here that popular opinion drew the line. The professional criminal class was defined first by its *refusal* to work and criminality then became the logical result of that decision.

In a curious way nineteenth-century moralisers harkened back to an earlier time when they discussed the question of crime. In the seventeenth century, crime was seen as a manifestation of the degradation of urban life, and writers always contrasted urban criminality and immorality with the purity and moral righteousness of the rural scene. They also drew direct comparisons between the nobility of rural labour – the sturdy yeoman – versus the deceit and deception that characterised urban business dealings. In the nineteenth century this tradition was resurrected, but on somewhat different terms. Now labour was venerated within the urban context; the honest 'workingman' became a moral ideal for all the members of the lower classes to emulate. The poor but honest labourer had his worst enemy in the inhabitant of the rookery where slothfulness and vice reigned supreme.

There was also another view of crime that emerged at this time. On the surface it appeared to be quite different from the attitudes just described, yet it flowed from the same basic premises. During the nineteenth century, many bourgeois writers began to blur the distinctions between the working poor and the criminal poor in order to explain the beginning of mass political agitation on behalf of the working class. In *Old Goriot* the criminal Vautrin remarks to Rastignac: 'There are only two courses to follow: stupid obedience or revolt.'³ The masses were beginning to challenge the political hegemony of the bourgeoisie. Yet they did not follow the pattern of previous political history in this respect. It had been the middle class, after all, that had used the rule of law in order to claim their own political rights. Yet it now appeared as though the working class was demanding its political freedom through the negation of law, or at least the negation of law and order. Observers perceived the degradation of working-class life as a self-fulfilling prophecy, and thus considered political violence and crime to be one and the same thing.

Contemporaries could thus approach the problem of crime from two different directions, but they were still dealing with two sides of the same coin. In essence the issue of criminality was part and parcel of the issue of discipline and social control. This had been a crucial part of the rationale for the criminal justice system in earlier times, but it now appeared that the system was breaking down. Personal crime and political crime both stemmed from the reluctance or refusal of the lower classes to respect authority and their denial of the moral and cultural restraints that justified the status quo. The split between the working and the non-working population had been accompanied by a split in the nature of crime. Each group committed its own kind; workers committed political crimes, non-workers committed personal crimes. The established classes would have to devise a particular method for dealing with each type. That is the subject of the following chapter.

CHAPTER 8

POLICE AND PUNISHMENT IN THE MODERN AGE

EUROPEAN society in the nineteenth century was now confronted by two types of violence – the violence connected with crime and the violence connected with politics. These phenomena had occurred before, but never in this particular manner. There had always been violent crime, but it had not been committed by a professional criminal class. There had always been outbreaks of political violence, but they had not been committed by mass groups organised around long-term political goals. Consequently, although the violence and disorder of this period may not have been quantitatively greater than in the past, its qualitative aspects were sometimes terrifying. As we stated in the previous chapter, the reaction of the established classes was to make little distinction regarding the question of crime. But having arrived at that consensus, the public still had to devise new methods to deal with the criminals. The method devised for dealing with political criminals was the police.

As late as the 1820s, the question of mass political violence remained distinct from the question of criminality. Yet political violence was becoming out of hand and the army seemed unable to handle large crowds of demonstrators in a peaceful manner. The most disquieting incident occurred in August 1819, when a crowd of more than 60,000 persons assembled for a day of speeches and demonstrations at St. Peter's Fields in Manchester. A single squad of hastily-deputised and amateurish

157

policemen proved unable to control the mob and this led to the summoning of the 15th Hussars to disperse the crowd. Their tactics resulted in eleven people killed and nearly six hundred wounded. The 'Peterloo Massacre', as it came to be known, demonstrated beyond a doubt that the new age of mass political agitation required new forms of mass control.

Ironically enough the authorities in Manchester in 1819 had first turned to the local policeman – the constable – and requested that he deal with the problem. The constable refused this request, and his refusal eventually brought the Hussars onto the scene. The constable had been the chief civilian law officer in England from the Middle Ages, but the Peterloo Massacre, along with other similar incidents, illustrated just how obsolete the office had become. As Reith remarks, 'the constable survived the Danish invasion, the Norman conquest, feudal conflict and the Wars of the Roses, the Reformation and the dissolution of the monasteries, the Civil War and the Restoration. He failed to survive and was extinguished by the Industrial Revolution.'[1]

The reason for the lengthy existence and the final disappearance of the constable was one and the same: it flowed directly from the role of the office and the nature of medieval and early modern police forces in general. The position of constable first arose in the thirteenth century, when the Norman conquerors strove to reorientate Saxon legal institutions toward new ends. The constable was elected by the members of each parish or manor, and he was required to supervise some of the activities of the tithing and organise the hue and cry. Since the constable was a royal officer his power grew alongside that of other Crown officials. His importance in the area of law enforcement was confirmed with the ascendancy of the Justices of the Peace. Yet it was precisely at this moment that the office began gradually to fall into disrepute. This was due largely to the fact that the office did not pay a salary, and most constables bought their way out of office by appointing a deputy who served in an equally desultory manner. Yet, until the nineteenth century, the office of the constable suited a society that remained essentially rural. Crime was still largely a private matter and mass movements were handled by detachments of the army or the guard.

What made the office of constable most ineffective, however, was the small number of officers compared to the general population. The population of Bradford, for example, numbered nearly 100,000 in the nineteenth century, but the police force consisted only of a Chief Constable, two assistants and one constable in each township. The city of Rochdale, already a large manufacturing town, had a police force of three persons plus a dozen night watchmen. The understaffing of police, particularly in rural zones, was not peculiar to England. In France, the whole Brie region and its urban centre of Meaux (with 6,500 persons) had a police force of four in the 1760s. The city of Chartres, which contained nearly 15,000 persons at the middle of the eighteenth century, had six police. The situation was no different in Spain. Often large villages of 3,000–4,000 persons had only two constables. Yet such pitiful numbers of law officers had sufficed even in cities until mass political violence presented the established classes with a crisis in law and order.

The development of a police system in response to political agitation was preceded and motivated by several other related events. In 1797 a Glasgow merchant-turned-magistrate, Patrick Colquhoun, published *A*

Treatise on the Police of the Metropolis. The book created a sensation; it went through seven editions in ten years and was translated into several foreign languages. The reaction to its appearance was not unlike the response that greeted Beccaria's work on criminal law. In many respects the book broke entirely new ground. First, the author insisted that the existence of a large police force did not constitute any threat to liberty, a point that the established classes were willing to concede in the light of recent events in revolutionary France. In the area of administration, Colquhoun proposed a complete separation of the police and the judiciary, the latter acting as a watchdog over the former. In the area of crime control, the author advocated the development of an organised intelligence service, the establishment of a register of notorious criminals, and the publication of a *Police Gazette* to inform the public about the latest happenings in crime and crime detection.

Colquhoun's theories were put to a practical test with the establishment of a Marine Police force in 1798. This was a group of salaried officers, supervised by Colquhoun and paid entirely out of a fund set up by London merchants who annually lost vast quantities of goods from the quays through plunder and pilferage. The force achieved such success in curbing river crime that the Thames River Act of 1800 established the Marine Police as a public body. Within the next decade, the city of London was finally subject to some degree of police security by the enlargement of these early police forces. Thus the development of the police was given further impetus by their effectiveness in curbing larceny and other forms of ordinary crime. And their ability to deal with political disturbances had increased as a result of the techniques employed on the river.

The police force was perfectly suited to maintaining security during periods of mass disturbances precisely because of the illegal and unethical tactics that it had always utilised to combat the criminal element. The energies of the mob could be contained if its leaders were closely watched, if their motives and plans were known, and if troublemakers were kept away from the scene. The police from earliest times had employed spies and informers – *mouchards* in Paris – who could learn any criminal scheme and divulge it for the proper price. It was thought better to arrest and illegally detain several known criminals than to risk an armed confrontation with a large and angry crowd. The police, as opposed to the army, specialised in adopting civilian mannerisms and dress in order to become part of the crowd that they had to control. This was a natural extension of their ability to don disguises to trap criminals who were also disguised. The appearance of the army at the scene of a demonstration was enough to provoke violence, while the police and their methods were hardly noticed by the crowd.

Yet despite the obvious advantages of using police to curb civil unrest while also allowing them to fight crime, a national police force did not develop rapidly in any European country. In 1829 Peel introduced a measure in the House of Commons to create a metropolitan police force in London, the same year that a city-wide police force began operating in Paris under the Prefect of Police, Louis-Marie Debelleyme. This was still, however, a far cry from a national force of law officers. The basis for such a development was laid in England in 1839 with the passage of the Rural Police Act. Even this legislation established only the structure of a nationwide law enforcement system; it did not immediately create a police force of sufficient size. Well into the 1840s and 1850s the police forces of England and the Continent remained quite small in relation to the population they were supposed to protect.

At the same time the size of the police in large cities grew quite rapidly. For this was where civil unrest and working-class violence had reached potent extremes. The inability to create a national force of any size was due to the reluctance of agriculturalists to subsidise an institution whose activities were more applicable to urban problems. When the national force was finally established, the proportion in the countryside was often ten times smaller than the proportion in cities. This gap remained well into the twentieth century. But at least the cities were now patrolled by an organised, uniformed force that studied and developed modern techniques for dealing with crime. As a result of the political problem, the bourgeoisie finally accepted the notion of a police force that operated in a variety of legal and illegal guises to curb political violence. These same methods would be sanctioned for dealing with other types of crime as well.

The appearance of the modern police force occurred concurrently with the development of modern punishment in the form of the penitentiary system. Like the police, the practice of imprisonment had developed in Europe at an earlier time, but would be adapted in a somewhat different form for modern use. This was not only because of the special requirements of modern punishment that could best be met within the context of a prison system. It also was a reflection of the gradual transformation in criminal punishment that had taken place in Europe.

Over the course of the fourteenth to the nineteenth centuries, five basic forms of punishment had been utilised in European criminal justice systems: execution,

physical brutality, monetary or other property confisca-
tion, banishment and imprisonment. All five types were
used concurrently and remained in use at the end of the
early modern period; but their relative effectiveness had
changed. Capital punishment was exercised infrequently
and in extreme cases only, largely because of moral considerations, and because convictions were much harder
to obtain without some alternate means of punishment.
Likewise corporal punishments were retained on the
statute books, but were also less frequently applied owing
to the moral, social and political realities of the time.
Monetary fines had proven to be totally unworkable since
more and more defendants appeared in court either
wholly or almost destitute; only the wealthier classes,
who rarely came before the courts, could afford to buy
their way out of the system. As has been discussed,
transportation was no longer a viable form of punishment after the nineteenth century. Of the five basic
forms of punishment, only imprisonment remained an
effective system by the end of the early modern period.

Punishment statistics published by Radzinowicz for
the early 1830s in England demonstrate the relative importance of each type of punishment. Of all persons sentenced in those years, more than 60 per cent received jail
terms. Transportation comprised slightly less than 25 per
cent of all sentences. Capital punishments totalled about
10 per cent of the total, although it is not clear how many
of those individuals had their sentences commuted.
Finally, corporal punishment and fines together constituted 3 per cent of the global figure.[2] These statistics
illustrate quite clearly the extent to which imprisonment
had become the dominant mode of punishment as
Europe entered the Industrial Age. In contrast we can
cite figures from Paris in the last part of the eighteenth

century, which show that imprisonment comprised only 10 per cent of the sentences, while banishment totalled more than 60 per cent and galley service comprised another 25 per cent of all punishments decreed by the court.[3]

Incarceration had been a form of forced segregation since before the early modern period. Originally it was conceived of in punitive terms, but it was also a method of guaranteeing that certain unreliable individuals would be available for trial or sentencing at the infrequent times that courts were in session. Pre-trial or pre-sentence detention was the basis of most incarceration until the sixteenth century. Henceforth incarceration took a different form. In 1555 an institution called the Bridewell opened in London for the purpose of incarcerating vagabonds and beggars. It was imitated throughout Europe and came to be known as the House of Correction, where persons unwilling to work would be forced to engage in socially useful labour. The early houses of correction thus began the tradition of accommodating the poorest elements in society, a characteristic which remained a hallmark of the penitentiary system to the present day.

Under the system adopted in England and the continent, inmate labour was used to produce marketable commodities, and the house of correction was run on a quasi-factory basis with staff collecting salaries based upon the profits from sales. Such a labour system became less practical, however, as free labour became more efficient. Many correctional institutions had been profitable only insofar as they were granted monopoly status, either in terms of purchase of raw materials or of sales of finished items. Once such monopolistic protection disappeared, as it did in many industries during the seventeenth and eighteenth centuries, costs of convict labour usually ran well ahead of returns. By the end of the seventeenth century the largest house of correction in France, the *Hôpital Général*, was running at an annual deficit of several hundred thousand *livres*. Nonetheless the idea of locking up indigents and forcing them to work had spread throughout Europe. Houses of correction were operating in every large French city by 1700, had been founded in Frankfurt and Spandau in the 1680s, and continued to open in German towns during the eighteenth century.

In the long run, however, the costs of such institutions would outweigh the benefits. Moreover the sort of people incarcerated would gradually change from paupers to all sorts of criminals. The houses of correction had been developed at a time when begging and vagrancy were considered serious crimes. Yet by the eighteenth century, criminality was defined in much wider terms and punishment was beginning to emerge in its modern, retributive context. Consequently the idea that prisoners should work while confined remained a central facet of prison organisation, even though the prison population was becoming more diverse. Furthermore, as other forms of punishment began to lose favour, the prison population swelled to an enormous degree. Conditions within specific institutions became chaotic, security was lax, petty brutality endemic and sanitation and health standards were non-existent. The situation in any particular prison usually reflected the degree of enterprise and initiative of the jailer. Some more energetic and committed jailers attempted to maintain a regular system of labour within their institutions and enforce a modicum of health and sanitary measures. But in many institutions the prison administration subsisted on bribes from inmates and payments from families to finance the purchase of necessary amenities.

By the beginning of the nineteenth century the combination of moral, social and economic circumstances would bring about a major reform of the prison system. The motivation behind this reform was clear. The criminal population was growing and there remained no other effective means of punishing so many. At the same time, the convict population was no longer producing products with enough marketability to support the costs of manufacture. If the state had to assume a larger portion of the costs of punishment, that particular punishment should at least embody either a high level of deterrence or have a highly punitive effect upon its victims. The disorder, filth and brutality that characterised prison life was hardly conducive to the creation of an environment in which punishment could be dealt out on an organised and effective basis. This had been the message in John Howard's *State of Prisons*, and the clamour that followed its publication in 1777 eventually led to the beginnings of real reforms.

Both English and continental reformers found their answer in the American penitentiary system and, in particular, the design of the Walnut Street Prison in Philadelphia. The most important element in the Walnut Street design was the use of solitary confinement where prisoners would eat, sleep and work within a single cell. This idea was also the basis for Jeremy Bentham's prison model, known as the Panopticon, although this was rejected by the parliamentary committee because its administration rested upon industrial profits. The Walnut Street Prison was visited in 1831 by de Tocqueville, who then returned to France and submitted a report that became the basis of the penitentiary plan adopted some fifteen years later.

The earliest type of reform came in the classification

and segregation of the prison population within a particular institution. In 1806 the jail at Bury adopted a ten-part classification system in which prisoners were divided by sex, type of offence (felony, misdemeanour or debt) and pre-trial or post-trial detention. The rationale behind this plan was provided by the idea that a hard-core criminal class should be kept distinct from casual criminals so that the latter would not be influenced to follow a career in crime. It was also hoped that segregation would bring some improvement in sanitation and health. Yet the problem of the effectiveness of incarceration still remained. If human beings were to be confined together for long periods, then every effort should be made to make their experiences completely uniform. This was the only way in which the period of incarceration could be used to instil discipline. In the wake of rising crime rates and widespread political agitation, nothing obsessed the upper classes more than the need to promote law and order through the maintenance of discipline. This was a basic theme of upper-class culture (*vido* Mrs. Gaskell's *Mary Barton*); it was also a strong element in religious thought, especially the Evangelical movement that began sending chaplains into all prisons. The advocates of personal regeneration through stern discipline found a perfect method in the separation of prisoners within the penal institution.

The development of a system of separate confinement largely accounts for the enormous number of brief prison sentences meted out in the nineteenth century. For it was believed that a short stay in solitude behind bars had a much more punitive and deterrent effect than a long sentence in a group institution. Alone and silent, the prisoner might reflect upon his criminal past in a more objective manner. He would have no support from his peers nor pressure to continue his unlawful ways. His mind would quickly rid itself of immoral (read: all) thoughts and would become a fertile field for religious and moral renewal. This was the philosophical basis for the emergence of the modern prison system.

All these ideas were incorporated in the Pentonville prison built and opened in London in 1840. Henry Mayhew visited the prison in 1862 and recorded his impressions.[4] Every cell was thirteen and a half feet long by seven and a half feet wide and nine feet high. It contained a water-closet and wash-basin, a three-legged stool, a table and gas-burner, and a hammock with a mattress and blankets. Every prisoner was given a number that referred to the location of his cell, and guards addressed prisoners by calling out their numbers; their proper names were never mentioned inside prison walls. All prisoners dressed exactly alike, their uniform including brown caps that covered the entire face except the eyes and mouth. The prison day began at 6 a.m. with breakfast at 7, followed by work in the cells, exercise in the yard, prayers and meals until 8.45. Prisoners were never allowed to converse with one another nor break the prison routine in any manner.

In essence the prison system, as it evolved in its modern form, linked the three basic aspects of modern punishment: brutality, anonymity and industry. This was a logical development given the evolution of criminal punishment throughout the early modern period. We recall that, in the Middle Ages, criminal justice was a method for settling personal disputes among persons of equal rank. Consequently there was no room in the system for excessive brutality. Feudal justice also rested upon a reciprocity of social relations based upon personal connections between adversaries in a criminal proceeding.

Therefore punishment could be anything but anonymous. Finally, since a crime in the feudal era was considered to be an attack by one person against another, punishment rested upon personal restitution, not social retribution. Consequently there was no need to perform retributive labour.

Over the course of the early modern period, the gradual transformation in punishment codes reflected the slow but steady evolution of a society based upon class divisions. As criminal punishment became a means of ensuring the hegemony of one class over another, its character was dramatically transformed and it was stripped of its medieval elements. Now punishment codes incorporated brutality on a regular basis as a means of teaching lessons to those who attacked their betters. As social distinctions grew between those who judged and those who were judged, and class justice replaced peer justice, so a large measure of anonymity surrounded all proceedings. At the same time, crime was now considered an assault on the social order. Consequently the criminal had to make restitution to the entire society by performing some form of work. In the eighteenth century all these factors began to operate in the criminal justice system in more obvious overt ways. The brutality of the system was exemplified by the enormous increase in capital punishments. The anonymity of the system was reflected in the increase in class distinctions between defendants and juries, and the disappearance of various methods (e.g. benefit of clergy) of reducing the seriousness of a particular plea. The necessity to produce in order to repay was one of the guiding principles behind the foundation of the House of Correction.

The modern prison combined these three factors, but in a special way that was possible only when society had arrived at the Industrial Age. In order to guarantee that every prisoner would receive the same treatment, it was imperative that total uniformity be imposed upon the prison population. Thus prisoners dressed exactly alike, were herded into identical cells, engaged in the same activities at the same time, ate the same food, sat on the same stools and stared at the same four walls. The key to a successful prison was discipline based upon regimentation, not profits. When operated efficiently, such a system was extremely brutal, although it left no physical scars. It reduced the felon to a state of complete anonymity. Finally, the prison population was regimented to work at endlessly repetitive tasks with no meaning beyond the drudgery of the labour itself.

When stripped to its barest essentials – brutality, anonymity, industry – the prison incorporated those same elements that were the hallmarks of the factory system. The relation of the felon to the prison system was a reproduction in the rawest sense of the relation of the worker to the factory. The worker was brutalised by noise; the prisoner was brutalised by silence. The worker was anonymous; his place on the line could be filled by another worker as quickly as the cell of one prisoner could be taken by another felon. The worker had to produce, but only in the prison was human labour alienated from production to a greater degree. The factory system and the prison system dealt with the same problem in two distinct but related ways. They imposed discipline upon the masses and rigidified the basic class divisions in society. Reduced to a similar state, the systems of labour and punishment had emerged in their modern forms.

CHAPTER 9
COMPARISON AND CONJECTURE

THE purpose of this book has been to relate changes in crime and punishment to changes in European society during the transition from the feudal to the capitalist age. Consequently, we have attempted to tie the pattern of crime and punishment to certain social, economic and political developments that occurred during that transitional period. The main theme of the work was that criminal activity and punishment systems reflected the relationship of various social classes to one another; that crime reflected the tensions inherent in those relationships, and that punishment was one response to those tensions. The reader may wonder, however, whether this explanation is historically valid, even if it appears to be logical. In other words, to what extent can changes in crime and punishment be made to fit exactly into a predetermined pattern of events? Some doubt must exist regarding the attempt to posit a direct, causal relationship between such disparate factors.

The first defence of this explanation rests upon the requirements of brevity. It was hardly possible to cover this vast topic and chronology without eliminating a wide variety of significant information. Many particular situations and unusual practices simply were left unmentioned due to the necessity of rendering a readable history of the entire problem within a relatively brief space. Therefore, I was faced with the choice of either creating a whole compendium of bits and pieces of information about

171

crime and punishment, a catalogue, or creating a work that would explain crime and punishment in a logical fashion. For obvious reasons I chose the latter course. But this choice was not made without precedent, of which the first and most important was the force of contemporary ideas. After ten years of studying and writing social history, I am convinced that the historian can find no better source than well-informed opinion. This can come from many sides, from both the bottom of society and from the top. No particular group has a monopoly on the world-view; rather, their view of the world reflects their relationship to it. What the upper classes saw as disorder, the lower classes saw as fun. What the lower classes experienced as misery, the upper classes experienced as the maintenance of law and order. There is no need to make value judgements about the evidence. The two positions are not contradictory; if understood dialectically, each one is proof of the validity of the other.

The point is that on all sides of the issue of crime and punishment, contemporaries usually viewed the question as it has been analysed in this book. Crime may have been defined differently at different times, but the definition was always closely related to society's conception of the social factors that provoked criminality. It was not crime *per se* that was feared, but the social conflicts and crises that spawned criminal behaviour. Consequently, many of the most important commentaries on crime and punishment did not address those issues directly. They spoke instead about all sorts of economic and social relations, but the implications were usually quite clear. Thus, when a true criminal reformer came on the scene and spoke directly to the issue of crime or punishment, his critiques of the problem were usually summations of developments that had already occurred. Beccaria's criticism of punishments, for example, was so forceful precisely because he provided an intellectual context for understanding rather than anticipating events. His proposal to abolish the death penalty was revolutionary in an intellectual sense, but it was also an acknowledgement that capital punishment was not working as a deterrent and was already falling into disuse.

A second defence of the theme of this book rests upon the coincidence of events. Both crime and punishment exhibited enormous chronological similarities between various European countries. Notwithstanding social, political and cultural lags, developments in one place were usually followed immediately by similar developments nearly everywhere else. Variations in crime statistics from different countries were usually more explainable in terms of statutory differences rather than actual criminal profiles. Criminal punishment systems and procedural devices were also remarkably similar and tended to change in the same manner at about the same time. These are not surprising findings. National borders and national cultures have never proven to be sufficient to prevent the formation of alliances of all sorts, both tacit and real. The ruling elite of one country took its cues from the experiences of other ruling groups, while the masses were also aware of the behaviour and experiences of their counterparts in other societies.

A third defence of the thesis of this work rests upon comparisons with areas of the world where economic and social developments were decidedly distinct from the history of Europe. If we look at the case for China, for example, we find that the situation reflected a society that was organised along much different lines, and would take a much different historical path into the modern world. The ancient Imperial dynasties began to impose a uniform system of criminal law and procedure throughout China as early as the Second Century B.C. This system, with many modifications and statutory revisions, remained intact over the entire course of dynastic history in China up to the last Ching Emperors. Thus, by the time the feudal law codes were first developed in Europe, the society of China had been governed by such codes for more than five hundred years. Moreover, while European feudal codes reflected the dispersal of authority into small, semi-autonomous local institutions, the Chinese codes reflected the concentration of political power atop a national, bureaucratic pyramid. As a result of this distinctive political structure, European and Chinese criminal codes were different from the beginning, and these differences would become greater over time.

Under Chinese law, as opposed to European feudal law, every criminal act was considered to be an attack upon state authority, and in theory the state could intervene in every criminal dispute. The plaintiff was either the actual victim or the state, and the process was initiated by denouncing the alleged culprit in a manner not dissimilar to the European system. Yet once the plaintiff entered a charge, he was duty-bound to prove that the event had occurred and that some actual damage had been suffered. The Chinese system placed great emphasis upon the ability of the plaintiff to prove his case in court, and failure to provide sufficient evidence to implicate the defendants could result in severe penalties for the plaintiff, his family and his associates. At the same time, the rendering of a guilty verdict not only placed the defendant in jeopardy, but could as well implicate his family, friends, associates, and even the inhabitants of his local neighbourhood. The penalties resulting from a guilty judgement were even applicable to later descendants of the original defendant.

In these respects, Chinese criminal procedure differed fundamentally from European feudal systems, since the former system placed great responsibility on the plaintiff to prove his charges, while the latter systems allowed the plaintiff to withdraw from the case almost at will. In fact, one of the first symptoms of legal modernisation in European criminal procedure occurred when statutes were enacted that either prohibited plaintiffs from withdrawing their charges prior to the disposition of a case, or removed the prosecution of a criminal case almost completely from private into public hands. Yet this emphasis upon the procedural intractability and the inability of the plaintiff to manipulate the system for personal ends would always remain a crucial feature of Chinese criminal codes.

Law and order was maintained in Chinese society through the *pao-chia*, a system that operated primarily as a method for collecting taxes, but also could be used to control crime. In the *pao-chia* system, every adult male belonged to a group of ten, all of whose members could be held responsible for the commission of a crime by any individual member of the group. This practice was somewhat similar to the English tithing system, although the latter practice usually served as a method of bond, while the *pao-chia* system was more directly related to the control of criminal activity. The tithing group was required to furnish ample reasons why any of its members did not appear in court during a criminal procedure, and its members could be assessed a fine if the court officer was not satisfied by the response. Under the *pao-chia* system, however, members of the group could be given the same sentence as the actual offender, whether or not the latter individual appeared in court. Like the tithing system, the *pao-chia* certainly reflected the fragmentation of rural life, the backwardness of social relations and the obvious necessity to maintain law and order within a small and semi-autonomous social unit. However, it also served as an effective method for maintaining discipline and order while deflecting people away from relying upon the public criminal system for settling disputes.

The rationale behind the severity and the collective responsibility imposed by the Chinese criminal justice system was provided by the needs of the Imperial government and the structure of the Imperial bureaucracy. Criminal justice in every county of China was administered by a Crown magistrate known as the *hsien-chang*, a royal officer whose exploits in the field of criminal detection were celebrated in the short stories of the ninth to twelfth centuries translated by Van Gulik. The office, or *yamen* of the *hsien-chang* was the lowest post in the imperial bureaucracy, but the *hsien-chang* had to perform successfully in that position in order to advance his public career. The post of *hsien-chang* was already operative by the eighth century and its functions remained the basic method for administering the county until the close of the Ching Dynasty. The office of the magistrate combined the duties of a tax-collector, judge, prosecuting attorney and coroner. Although the magistrate could and did farm out these activities to others, employing subalterns as tax officials and local constables, he remained legally responsible for faithfully discharging all official duties. Magistrates were rotated from county to county every three years, and never served in the province of their birth. More importantly, rapid advancement in the Imperial bureaucracy required that the magistrate complete all official tasks prior to the end of his three-year term. When a magistrate closed his books for the last time, all taxes had to be collected, all crimes had to be solved. Any unfinished business was a reflection of the incompetence of the particular administrator.

As a result of the pressures upon the *hsien-chang* to render the duties of his office as effectively as possible, every magistrate endeavoured to settle most issues in an unofficial capacity. By guaranteeing that any use of public procedure entailed grave risks for all parties concerned, the magistrate discouraged official entanglements in most criminal affairs. Aside from murder, which automatically became a matter of Imperial inquiry, most other criminal disputes could be settled in consultations between the magistrate and the local gentry, the latter relying upon village elders and clan heads to aid in keeping the peace. The social structure of the Chinese settlement – the great division in wealth and status – enabled many clan heads and village notables to maintain law and order through the use of private, unofficial peacekeeping forces. Only at times of extreme crisis would local village rulers call in the public authorities. Chinese criminal law was sometimes used as a brutal means of insuring support for such Confucian doctrines as status, filial piety and discipline, but nearly everyone in Chinese society had a vested interest in keeping disputes outside the official channels.

As we have seen in the case of Europe, the emergence of modern criminal systems would result in the attempt to legalise every criminal dispute and bring each incident under the purview of the official system. Thus, although the Chinese began with a theoretical adherence to state authority, the actual procedure avoided the use of this authority whenever possible. In Europe the system began with no attention paid either theoretically or realistically to state power, but ultimately evolved into a system held together by the force and authority of the national state. Yet as we have seen, the appearance of the state within the context of European criminal justice was as much a reflection of certain economic and social pressures as it was a reflection of specific political developments. I believe that most of the social and economic factors arose precisely because of the transformation of Europe to an industrial society.

It is not possible to conclude this work without drawing some further implications from the evidence or lack of evidence and posing a brief series of conjectures. The reader will notice an almost invariable use of the masculine pronoun when discussing crime or criminals in the text. This was not only done for syntactical reasons. The reality of the situation is that women rarely appeared as defendants in criminal cases. In sixteenth-century Essex they comprised only 10 per cent of all defendants, and numbered less than 15 per cent of all defendants in seventeenth-century rural Spain. In urban areas the figure was somewhat higher, reaching 20 per cent in pre-revolutionary Paris. Notwithstanding the fact that these statistics neglect certain types of criminality peculiar to women (e.g., witchcraft), it is still quite clear that their numbers in criminal cases not only ran far below their actual proportion of the population, but also below their proportion of the criminal population. The factors that would explain this great discrepancy are not clear. We could present some obvious possibilities, such as the role structure of society, the reluctance to remove women from the home, and the more covert nature of their crimes. But with the exception of sexual crime, this is an area that is totally unexplored.

The reader might also suspect that by defining crime in its social context, one could easily romanticise its various elements. There could be no greater misreading of my intentions. When all is said and done, crime is crime, and that banal fact should be remembered by all who study the subject. Although a logical explanation can be offered for the appearance of a *lumpen* class, that should not obscure the fact that such a class existed for the purpose of committing crime. And although some of their activities were seen as necessary, if obnoxious expedients for the rational functioning of the social order, every member of that social order had to take steps to protect himself against the ravages of the criminal class. I have spent chapters detailing the development of formal criminal law and procedures as exercised by and on behalf of the upper classes. But we have not said one word about the informal methods adopted by the masses to protect themselves. This is another issue that poses endless horizons.

This brings me directly to my third and final conjecture. It might appear that by distinguishing between workers and *lumpen* I am creating a social difference that in reality did not exist. As mentioned in the text, it is misleading to draw the line too firmly between any social groups. But in attempting to discuss cultural and behavioural differences between various strata of the masses, I do not mean any exoneration of their condition. The dialectical relationship between rich and poor was based upon exploitation, and this exploitation was often answered through the medium of crime. It is precisely for this reason that the criminal justice system appears sometimes to be so tolerant of crime – toleration disguises exploitation.

After writing nearly several hundred pages with the purpose in mind of explaining the historical logic behind crime and punishment, I would like to end this text by offering one illogical note. I have used the word 'system' throughout the book to describe criminal procedure and punishment, and by this I mean a planned, comprehensive method for dealing with the problem. But I also have a different meaning in mind. For once a system is established, in this as in anything else, it feeds off its own structure. The police need criminals to chase, the courts need criminals to judge, the prisons need criminals to punish. There is something about the inevitability of the entire system that transcends questions of history and logic. This brings us back to the statement of Sir Thomas More at the beginning of the book. We cannot escape his argument. In this respect, crime and punishment represent the development of modern society to its greatest degree.

NOTES AND GUIDE TO FURTHER READING

Until recently, crime and punishment were marginal subjects in European historiography, and they were usually raised as incidental topics on the edge of other, more important themes. Consequently, many of the arguments and observations in the text are derived from sources that have no concrete bearing upon questions treated here. Many of the points discussed in the text are also drawn from contemporary accounts, both historical and literary. With few exceptions, the bibliography appended here does not list either of these categories. Rather, it is comprised only of those secondary works that directly treat the problems of crime and punishment in historical terms. It has also been our intention, if at all possible, to confine the bibliography to works printed in English, and to avoid primary or archival sources that would be beyond the reach of most students. The suggestions for further reading, therefore, form an introductory guide to the bibliography on a subject whose historical dimensions are just now being appreciated.

INTRODUCTION

1. M. Foucault, *Discipline and Punish, The Birth of the Prison* (New York, 1977), p. 42.
2. N. Castan, *Justice et répression en Languedoc à l'époque des lumières* (Paris, 1980), p. 147.

Further Reading

It would be impossible to list all the works that have been published on aspects of popular unrest and revolutions in early modern Europe. The following list comprises only several of the generally-accepted syntheses of the literature: R. Mousnier, *Peasant Furies and Peasant Revolts in the Seventeenth Century* (New York, 1968), G. Rude, *The Crowd in History, Popular Disturbances in England and France, 1730–1848* (New York, 1964), E. J. Hobsbawm, *Primitive Rebels* (London, 1959), G. A. Williams, *Artisans et sans culottes, Popular Movements in France and Britain during the French Revolution* (London, 1968). E. P. Thompson raises a different perspective on the motives of rioters in, 'The Moral Economy of the English Crowd in the Eighteenth Century,' *Past and Present*, 50 (Feb., 1971), pp. 76–136, and Geoffrey Parker examines the question of military crime in, 'Mutiny and Discontent in the Spanish Army of Flanders, 1572–1607,' *Past and Present*, 58 (Feb., 1973), pp. 38–52. On the question of witchcraft, the reader might consult, A. Macfarlane, *Witchcraft in Tudor and Stuart England* (London, 1970), E. W. Monter, *Witchcraft in France and Switzerland* (Ithaca, 1976), and H. C. Midelfort, *Witch Hunting in Southwestern Germany, 1562–1684*. One should also consult the relevant sections in, K. Thomas, *Religion and the Decline of Magic* (New York, 1971). For studies of political crimes, any list should include, R. Mousnier, *The Assassination of Henry IV* (London, 1973), and G. Marañon, *Antonio Perez, 'Spanish Traitor'* (London, 1954).

CHAPTER I

1. *Autobiography of Benvenuto Cellini,* trans. by John Addington Symonds (New York, 1961), pp. 124–28.
2. The individuality of rural violence was not characteristic of homicide. In England during the thirteenth century, nearly 70% of all persons accused of homicides in eyre courts named companions who were somehow involved in the affair. See J. Given, *Society and Homicide in Thirteenth-Century England* (Stanford, 1977).
3. L. Martines, ed., *Violence and Civil Disorder in Italian Cities, 1200–1500* (Berkeley, 1972), and M.-T. Lorcin, 'Les paysans et la justice dans la région Lyonnaise aux XIVe et XVe siècles,' *Moyen Age,* LXXIV, 2 (1968), pp. 269–300. A recent work presents comprehensive figures for criminal indictments in England, 1300–1348. The overall distribution was as follows:

Larceny	38.7%
Burglary	24.3
Homicide	18.2
Receiving	6.2
Misc.	2.1

From, B. Hanawalt, *Crime and Conflict in English Communities, 1300-1348* (Cambridge, Mass., 1979), p. 66. The evidence deals largely with rural crime and excludes assaults, which were not indictable offences in country criminal courts.

Further Reading

There is a wealth of literature covering economic and social developments during the Middle Ages. Some of the best general works are: H. Pirenne, *Economic and Social History of Medieval Europe* (London, 1936); M. Bloch, *French Rural History: an essay on its basic characteristics* (London, 1966); B. H. Slicher von Bath, *The Agrarian History of Western Europe, A.D. 500–1850* (London, 1963); and a recent survey of the literature, N. J. G. Pounds, *An Economic History of Medieval Europe* (London, 1974). These works illustrate the enormous diversity of medieval social and economic institutions. On the question of crime during the period, the Martines collection cited above contains several important contributions, especially the articles by Werner Gundersheimer, 'Crime and Punishment in Ferrara,' and Stanley Chojnacki, 'Crime, Punishment and the Trecento Venetian State'. The reader should also note the works by Given and Hanawalt cited above.

CHAPTER II

1. John P. Dawson, *A History of Lay Judges* (Cambridge, Mass. 1960), p. 301.
2. Historically, formal criminal procedures were adopted as a means of inhibiting feud. Early procedure, particularly in Germanic areas, had the effect of transforming armed combat into legal combat, and this process became commonplace throughout Europe by the thirteenth century. See F. Helie, *Traité de l'instruction criminelle* (Paris, 1845), pp. 506–40.
3. This does not mean that early procedure was devoid of strict rules of conduct. One scholar has characterised the process as, 'public, oral and formal.' See A. Tardif, *La procédure civile et criminelle aux XIIIe et XIVe siècles* (Paris, 1885), p. 1.

4. *Archivo Municipal*, Toledo, Section: *Causas Criminales*, no. 1432.
5. Pre-trial detention appears to have been common in England from at least 1166, according to Ralph Pugh, *Imprisonment in Medieval England* (Cambridge, 1968).

Further Reading

The subject of punishment and criminal law during the Middle Ages still awaits a comprehensive treatment but the multiplicity of jurisdictions and legal privileges will probably discourage most scholars from tackling the problem in a direct fashion. Nonetheless, there are certain sources that should be consulted. For England, the indispensable work remains Sir Frederick Pollock and Frederick W. Maitland, *The History of English Law*, 2 vols. (Cambridge, 1898). An interesting recent addition to the literature is J. Bellamy, *Crime and Public Order in England in the Later Middle Ages* (London, 1973). Unfortunately, there does not exist a detailed study of Germanic feudal law in English, and many of the specialised, older studies (Stobbe, DuBoys) have not been reprinted in modern editions. They are summarised, however, in the important work of A. Esmein, *A History of Continental Criminal Procedure* (Boston, 1913), and the less-satisfactory study by Carl Ludwig von Bar, *A History of Continental Criminal Law* (Boston, 1916).

CHAPTER III

1. R.H. Tawney, 'An Occupational Census of the Seven-

teenth Century,' *Economic History Review*, V (1934), pp. 25–64, reprinted in J. M. Winter (ed.) *R. H. Tawney: The American Labour Movement and other Essays* (Hassocks, 1979).
2. W. G. Hoskins, 'The Rebuilding of Rural England, 1570–1640,' *Past and Present*, 4 (1953), p. 44.
3. Joel Samaha, *Law and Order in Historical Perspective, the Case of Elizabethan Essex* (New York, 1974), and, Michael Weisser, *The Peasants of the Montes* (Chicago, 1977).
4. Pierre Vilar, *La Catalogne dans l'Espagne moderne*, I (Paris, 1962), p. 581.

Further Reading

Bibliography covering the economic and social structures of early modern Europe is extensive, and we will cite only several of the most basic sources. Carlo Cipolla has contributed a number of important works to this field, of which an important study is *Before the Industrial Revolution* (New York, 1976). For England, a concise view of the problem is found in J. D. Chambers, *Population, Economy and Society in Pre-Industrial England* (London, 1972). For Spain and Italy there is still no work to compare with Fernand Braudel, *The Mediterranean and the Mediterranean World during the Epoch of Philip II*, 2 vols. (London, 1972). An interesting summary of recent literature is provided by Immanuel Wallerstein, *The Modern World-System, Capitalist Agriculture and the Origins of the European World-Economy in the Sixteenth Century* (New York, 1974). We do not yet possess any major synthesis of criminal statistics for the early modern period, but along with the works cited in note 3, a number of specialised studies have recently appeared. For England, there is an important collection of essays edited by J. S. Cockburn, *Crime in England, 1500–1800* (London, 1977). For the situation in France, there are several studies of crime and criminality in different areas of Normandy, published in *Annales de Normandie* by students of Pierre Chaunu. See the articles by B. Boutelet on the bailliage of Pont de l'Arche (*Annales de Normandie*, 12 (1962), pp. 235–262; by J. C. Gegot on the bailliage of Falaise (*ibid.*, 16 (1966), pp. 103–64; by M. M. Champin on the bailliage of Alençon and by A. Margot on the bailliage of Mamers (*ibid.*, 22 (1972), pp. 47–84 and 185–224). All four articles however, are based on relatively few cases per head of the population. For Spain, the article by Ruth Pike, 'Crime and Punishment in XVIth Century Spain' *The Journal of European Economic History*, 5, 3 (Winter 1976), pp. 689–705 is inadequate, but at least it points the reader toward an appreciation of picaresque literature. The latter subject is admirably treated in a new text by Harry Sieber, *The Picaresque* (London, 1977).

CHAPTER IV

Further Reading

The subject of criminal law and procedure in the early modern period has lately attracted its share of attention. For England, a very intelligent work on criminal administration is J. S. Cockburn, *A History of English Assizes from 1558 to 1714* (Cambridge, 1972). This book should be read in companion with John P. Dawson's work cited in Chapter II, and the brief summary by E. Moir, *The Justice of the Peace* (London, 1969). For France, the basic work remains Esmein, but it should be supplemented by the brilliant comparative study of John Langbein, *Prosecuting Crime in the Renaissance, England, Germany, France* (Cambridge, Mass., 1974). For Spain, the subject is adequately treated by Francisco Tomas y Valiente, *El derecho penal de la monarquía absoluta* (Madrid, 1969). Despite the attention paid to Renaissance legal institutions by Martines, Becker and others, there still remains no modern text on the subject of criminal law to displace the early summary by Carlo Calisse, *History of Italian Law* (Boston, 1928).

CHAPTER V

1. J. M. Beattie, 'The Pattern of Crime in England, 1600–1800,' *Past and Present*, 62 (Feb. 1974), pp. 47–95.

Further Reading

There are numerous surveys of European society in the eighteenth century, and the reader can find these sources with ease. One interesting perspective, however, is found in sections of Fernand Braudel, *Capitalism and Material Life* (London, 1973). The reader should also consult D. George, *London Life in the Eighteenth Century* (London, 1935). Crime in the eighteenth century has been the subject of a number of interesting studies. A group of essays on England has been edited by E. P. Thompson, *Albion's Fatal Tree* (London, 1975), and the reader is directed most particularly to the contributions by Cal Winslow, 'Sussex Smugglers,' and Douglas Hay, 'Property, Authority and the Criminal Law.' A more detailed study of property and criminality is E. P. Thompson, *Whigs and*

Hunters (London, 1975). An interesting collection of essays covering France is edited by F. Billacois, *Crimes et criminalité en France* (Paris, 1971), but the reader should not miss relevant portions of O. Hufton, *The Poor of Eighteenth-Century France* (Oxford, 1974).

CHAPTER VI

1. A. Manzoni, *Tho Column of Infamy*, od. by A. P. d'Entrèves (London, 1964).
2. As quoted in, M. Maestro, *Cesare Beccaria and the Origins of Penal Reform* (Philadelphia, 1973), p. 33.
3. There have been numerous editions of Beccaria published in every Western language. The most lucid introduction is found in the work of F. Venturi (Turin, 1975).
4. Figures on punishments at the Old Bailey are as follows:

Year	Death	Trans.	Whipping	Prison
1760–64	12.7%	74.1	12.3	1.2
1765–69	15.8	70.2	13.4	0.8
1770–74	17.0	66.5	14.2	2.3
1775–79	20.7	33.4	17.6	28.6

   See, M. Ignatieff, *A Just Measure of Pain, The Penitentiary in the Industrial Revolution* (New York, 1978), p. 81.
5. Charles Dickens, *Oliver Twist* (modern edn. New York, 1961), p. 476.

Further Reading

General approaches to eighteenth-century penal theories are provided by Leon Radzinowicz, *Ideology and Crime*

(London, 1966), and J. Heath, *Eighteenth-Century Penal Theory* (Oxford, 1963). Although there are several intelligent studies of Beccaria, surprisingly little has been published on the social implications of his thought. John Langbein contributes an interesting argument in *Torture and the Law of Proof* (Chicago, 1977), but confines his study to the legal aspects of the problem. Galley slaves and punishment is studied by Paul Bamford, *Fighting Ships and Prisons: The Mediterranean Galleys of France in the Age of Louis XIV* (Minneapolis, 1973).

CHAPTER VII

1. F. Engels, *The Condition of the Working Class in England* (modern edn. Stanford, 1968), p. 71.
2. Charles Dickens, *Martin Chuzzlewit* (modern edn. Baltimore, 1968), p. 187.
3. H. Balzac, *Old Goriot* (London, 1935), p. 87.

Further Reading

There is an immense literature on the economic and social changes that accompanied European industrialisation. Works cited here are those which discuss aspects of the problem particularly relevant to crime and punishment. In that respect, an interesting approach is taken by Charles Morazé, *The Triumph of the Middle Classes* (London, 1966). Although the interpretation of certain social developments differs widely from parts of our text, the reader must consult E. P. Thompson, *The Making of the English Working Class* (London, 1966). For a general orientation to the problems of crime and society, the reader should see Louis Chevalier, *Laboring Classes and*

Dangerous Classes In Paris During the First Half of the Nineteenth Century (New York, 1973). A more specific analysis is provided by J. Tobias, *Crime and Industrial Society in the 19th Century* (New York, 1967). The reader will also notice that portions of this chapter rely upon the compelling observations of Henry Mayhew, whose work, *London Labour and London Poor* has been reissued in a modern version (New York, 1968). Many of the points raised in this chapter can also be pursued with reference to the bibliography for Chapter VIII.

CHAPTER VIII

1. C. Reith, *The Blind Eye of History* (Montclair, 1975), p. 29.
2. L. Radzinowicz, *History of the English Criminal Law*, I (London, 1948), pp. 143–44.
3. P. Petrovitch, 'Recherches sur la criminalité à Paris dans la seconde moitié du XVIIIe siècle,' *Crimes et criminalité en France* (Paris, 1971), p. 227.
4. H. Mayhew and J. Binny, *The Criminal Prisons of London* (modern edn. New York, 1968), pp. 112–72.

Further Reading

Recent research has begun to uncover many aspects of the development of penal institutions and police. Regarding the former, the latest work is by Michel Foucault, *Discipline and Punish, The Birth of the Prison* (New York, 1977), which follows from some of his ideas expressed in *Madness and Civilization* (New York, 1965). Also see the significant new work by Michael Ignatieff cited above. The early history of incarceration is covered in Thorsten Sellin,

Pioneering in Penology: The Amsterdam Houses of Correction in the Sixteenth and Seventeenth Centuries (Philadelphia, 1944). The reader should also not overlook the important piece by U. R. Q. Henriques, 'The Rise and Decline of the Separate System of Prison Discipline,' *Past and Present*, 54 (February 1972), pp. 61–93. On the police, a very relevant discussion can be found in F. C. Mather, *Public Order in the Age of the Chartists* (Manchester, 1959). The early history of the London police force is sketched by Wilbur Miller, *Cops and Bobbies, Police Authority in New York and London, 1830–1870* (Chicago, 1977). Concerning crime in China, the reader may refer with profit to the study of D. Bodde and C. Morris, *Law in Imperial China* (Harvard, 1967). For two recent examples of how to exploit the full wealth of criminal court records, see: Yves Castan, *Honnêté et relations sociales en Languedoc, 1715–1780* (Paris, 1974), and T. R. Gurr, P. N. Grabosky and R. C. Hula, *The Politics of Crime and Conflict: A Comparative History of Four Cities* (London, 1977). For the problems which dog attempts to establish 'crime-rates' for pre-industrial societies, see T. Sellin and M. E. Wolfgang, *The Measurement of Delinquency* (New York, 1964), and B. Lenman and G. Parker, 'The State, the Community and the Criminal Law in Europe, 1250–1850', in V. A. C. Gatrell, B. Lenman and G. Parker (eds)., *Crime and the Law since 1500: Historical Essays* (London, 1979).

INDEX